ENCYCLOPEDIA OF SCALES
FOR HARMONICA

David Herzhaft

Cover: Haroula Kontorousi
Photos : Olesja Martin

ISBN - 978-1494954383

No part of this publication may be reproduced in any form or by any means without the prior written permission of the Publisher
© Musicoland LLC, PO Box 6747, 91365 WOODLAND HILLS 2013 © Harmonica School
International Copyright Secured - All rights reserved
visit us at : www.encyclopediaofscales.com

CONTENTS

Presentation	3
How to use Scales?	11
7 Note Scales:	17
Major Scale	18
Minor Melodic Scale	23
Minor Harmonic Scale	27
Major Harmonic Scale	31
Double Minor Harmonic	35
5 Note Scales:	39
Pentatonic Scales (Major and Minor)	40
Blues Pentatonic Scale (Blues Scale)	44
m7b5 Pentatonic Scale	48
Dominant Pentatonic Scale (Minor 6 Scale)	52
Symmetrical Scales:	56
Chromatic	57
Whole tone	58
Half-Diminished (or Diminished)	60
Augmented	62
Extras scales:	
Bebop	66
Extra Scales	69
Extra Pentatonic Scales	73
Appendix :	
Intervallic Formulas	77
Chord-Scale Relation Chart	80

Encyclopedia of Scales for the Harmonica

Presentation

This book provides you with the most useful scales in music. This book should help you learn scales faster, they are written in standard music notation suitable for diatonic and chromatic harmonica as well as in diatonic harmonica tabs format.

Each scale type is explained and played on the extra DVD so that you can hear its unique sound on a harmonica, and in a musical context, you can then practice it on the playback tracks that you can download for free from **www.encyclopediaofscales.com**. Useful tips are given so that you can learn and apply those scales faster and more accurately. Notating scales, and memorizing them can really be a pain in the art of playing harmonica. We hope this book will make the job easier and be a reference book to your harmonica playing.

What is a Scale ?

A scale is a series of tones, usually we call scale a group of at least 5 different tones As there are 12 tones it is very easy to randomly, and mathematically create a scale, give it a try!

However the purpose of this book is to give you a collection of the main scales used in music, from Traditional styles to Jazz and Classical music. We also added some extra less common scales for the curious. It is our aim thus to offer you the most comprehensive, and useful choice of scales adapted to the harmonica.

Scales and Modes

A scale could be considered as the most important reference of a series of tones and that's why it gets the status of "scale". A mode is simply another scale derived from within a main scale.

Let's explain the concept better:

If we would consider numbers as notes then we could say that **1234567** is called the major scale but that **2345671** would be called **Dorian** mode, the Dorian mode is what we call a mode, it is in reality a scale found within the major scale.
C Major scale aka C Ionian: CDEFGABC

Now if we start on the second note D we get:

D Dorian : DEFGABCD

Same notes, but the root change, and as we move on the second degree of the major scale playing those notes in this order, yield a totally different sound than the major scale. Every time we're going to move up a degree in the scale and change the root we will get a new mode and new sound, BUT, we're still using the exact same notes **CDEFGABC**, the order and root change creates a different sound!

The Modes

Here is the list of the modes of the major scale. The example is in the key of C to make it easier to learn. We will use those names as reference for the book.

From each scale we will get as many modes as there are notes. So for any note scale we have 7 modes.

Major Scale:

C Ionian (usually called C major scale): CDEFGABC
D Dorian: DEFGABCD
E Phrygian: EFGABCDE
F Lydian: FGABCDEF
G Mixolydian: GABCDEFG
A Aeolian: ABCDEFGA
B Locrian: BCDEFGAB

Some modes are really considered by improvisers to be as important as the main scale and you will find audio examples on the DVD for those, but the layout being exactly the same as the main scale, there is really no reason to repeat the notation and learn a new scale/diagram.

If you want to learn your D Dorian mode notes on a C Harmonica, simply have a look at the C major scale and play it from the D note instead of starting on the C.

The 3 main scales: major, melodic minor and harmonic minor, have 7 different modes each. We will give you information about those and how to use the notation to work on the most important ones, but there is really no need to repeat tab and notation for each mode once you understood the process.

Scales and Harmonica

A major difficulty for the harmonica player is to play in different keys, each key creates technical issues that the harmonica player has to deal with in the best possible way and it can turn into a mouth-ache in no time.

To help you work on your scales and master them, we will give you each scale in 12 different keys for a Harmonica in C. Working on a C harmonica is a good habit, since the C harmonica is right in the middle range between the G (lower) and the F (higher). Moreover, C has the simplest layout of notes.

Different Harmonicas?

If you play the C major scale on a C harmonica, it will be the same as if you would play an A major scale on an A harmonica. If you play a D major scale on a C harmonica it will be the same as if you would play a B major scale on an A harmonica.

We're not going to write down all 12 keys for the 12 usual harmonica keys because if you know a scale in 12 keys on a C harmonica, then you know them on any harmonica, you just have to transpose.

Diatonic, Chromatic and Tabs?

Most chromatic harmonica players know how to read music and that's good for them! Most diatonic players don't and that's really too bad! I hope that working with this book will give you an opportunity to understand that it is so much better to use music notation than tabs, and you should know your notes everywhere on your harmonica.

A 10 hole diatonic harmonica will cover the exact same range as a 12 hole chromatic harmonica, so if you know how to read music, this book works out for both models!

Practice?

First of all it is mandatory to know where the notes are on your instrument, as scales are composed of intervals, I also suggest that you learn your intervals by heart, only then you can start learning the notes of each scale.

For example, if you want to play D major or any of its related modes you should know right away that D major is **DEF#GABC#** without having to even think about it, that's why I suggest you to learn one scale at a time, and practice it in a lot of various ways before proceeding to a new scale. There's a limited number of scales and you're going to use some of them more often than others anyways, so simply start by working on the one you're interested in first and try to know them thoroughly.

If you need to quick check a scale no problem the book is meant for that. If you plan on improving your harmonica skills then go slowly and tackle one scale/sound at a time, since the Harmonica is in C and has only non-altered tones when you blow or draw notes. My approach is to learn only the altered notes of each scale, this is very effective and will make your life simpler.

I consider that I can play all notes by default: **CDEFGAB**, then if I think about A major I think to specifically replace **F, C** and **G** by **F# C# G#.**

For D melodic minor I think C# = I think to play all the notes but the C gets # all the time, so D melodic minor could be seen as C major scale with a C# instead of C. It works well when you have 2 or 3 altered notes but gets more complicated when you have 4, 5 or 6 alterations, when it happens I usually think the opposite way.

Db major for example, I don't think to play all 5 flat notes **Bb Eb Ab Eb Gb**, I think I'm going to play only altered notes (it doesn't really matter here if you think # or b) except for C and F, so if I start from the bottom I'm going to play C, then Db, then Eb, then F, then Gb, then Ab, and Bb, and I know that the easiest notes for me to play are the C and F because I get them naturally on the harmonica.

So for each scale and this is particularly important for major, melodic and harmonic scales I rely on alterations. Some people consider the melodic minor scale as a major scale with a minor third, and this is an interesting way of seeing it, but I don't find this approach useful for the harmonica. As whenever we transpose the math's become more and more complicated. For me it is just easier/faster to know the alterations and intervallic formula. If I think D minor melodic, I don't think D major DEF#GABC# and flat the third, I just think C# or 12b34567.

The ultimate goal is not to think but to play what you hear. Feel free to use whatever approach works best for you.

The different Keys Layout Choice:

When you learn a scale you don't want to learn it in a close-minded way, on the opposite you want to understand and learn it in an open way so that you can use this scale in a lot of different situations and have a great knowledge of it. That's why we use a global layout system instead of a root to root system.

For example, if you take a look at the G major scale: GABCDEF#G, we should start from the G (hole 2 draw), but then what about the lower notes down to hole 1? Picture having a good visual image of your scale on your harmonica is key to the success of learning those scales.
I then encourage you to get a full representation/diagram of scales instead of a gated view. The layout is made so that you will see the full range of the scale on your harmonica from bottom to top. As we've stated earlier in the mode explanation, the only thing you have to do to get your scale sound the way you want, is to start on the root.
So for the G major scale even though the notation starts on the C, you would start on the G to make it sound G major. Nonetheless, as soon as possible you should experiment playing in all the different areas of your harmonica and only landing/resolving your scale on the root to make it sound properly.

If you would like to make G major sound as A Dorian you would then use the exact same diagram but this time start or land on the A note. If you would like to make it sound as D Mixolydian, you would play the same notes and use the same diagram but use the D as the main root tone.

I hope that you now understand how powerful it is to learn and see your harmonica like this, rather than learning and having one diagram for G major, one for A Dorian, one for D Mixolydian and so on...

Playback and Examples on the DVD

Instead of just writing a book full of notes and tab we thought it would be more musical and interesting for your ears, and practice, to include audio examples for each scale family as well as playback to practice. The audio example will help you to hear the essence of the scale, and might also help you to get some starting point ideas. The playback tracks will let you try the scale and get a hold of it!
Download the playback tracks for free at **www.encyclopediaofscales.com**

The extra info is available on the DVD sold separately!

Scales and Intervallic Numbering

To learn and understand scales faster, we will use a very common system, Numbers for Intervals:

1: Fundamental
b2: Flat Second
2: Second
b3: Minor Third
3: Major Third
4: Perfect Fourth
#4 or b5: Sharp Fourth/Flat Fifth
5: Fifth
#5 or b6: Sharp Fifth or Flat Sixth
6: Sixth
b7: Minor Seventh
7: Major Seventh
8: Octave

I recommend you also train your ears to hear those intervals; The major scale that we all know is then labeled:

12345678 or **1234567** (8 is just a repetition of the 1 an octave higher)

Chords

I refer to chords in this book so here are a the intervallic formulae's for the main chord types as well as the relative chord in C:

Major Triad: 135 => CEG
Minor Triad: 1b35 => CEbG
Diminished Triad: 1b3b5 => CEbGb
Augmented Triad: 13#5 => CEG#
Sus 2 Triad: 125 => CDG
Sus 4 Triad: 145 => CFG
Maj 7: 1357 => CEGB
7: 135b7 => CEGBb
Min7: 1b35b7 => CEbGBb
Min7b5: 1357 => CEGB
MinMaj 7: 1b357 => CEbGB
Maj6: 1356 => CEGA
Min6: 1b356 => CEbGA
7b5: 13b5b7 => CEGbBb
7#5: 13#5b7 => CEG#Bb
Maj7#5: 13#57 => CEG#B

Alt: implies #5 and usually a b9 or #9, there are different ways to create an altered chord, here is one: **13#5b7b9 => CEG#BbDb**

Extensions: 9 – 11 – 13

Those are repetition of the 2, 4 and 6 an octave higher; you can choose to add extension on any chord, once you do so you make the scale related to the chord more obvious.

For example, over a **Cmaj7 CEGB** you can play the C major scale, or C Lydian or C Ionian augmented, but over Cmaj7#11 the C major scale will sound flat as it does not have a #4.
Whenever you play with a bass player you don't have to play the root, and can lighten the chord, you can also very often omit the 5 as it is common to most chords and don't really define the chord (unless the chord has a b5 or #5). The most important notes over any chord are the third and seventh. In a progression they are called guide tones.

Fake – Repetitive Scales

As we've seen so far a scale is a mathematic combination of intervals, let's take the exotic double harmonic minor scale: **12b3#45b67**

Now let's say you open a cool book of scales and you find this:

Double harmonic major scale … And you start to think … hmm why this scale is not in my encyclopedia? Cool down, I like to save paper, the double harmonic major scale is: **1b2345b67**

Now let's build Fm double harmonic minor: **FGAbBCDbE,**
And let's build C double harmonic major : **CDbEFGAbB**
C double major harmonic = **F double harmonic minor**

Well, I just saved you a dozen of "new scales" to learn, you will find a bunch of super exotic names for scales, just do the math and most of the time you will find that the new scale is just a mode derived from a regular scale. Then exoticism vanishes as fast as a processed guacamole in a can.

List of Scales in This Book

- Major
- Minor melodic
- Minor harmonic
- Major Harmonic
- Double minor harmonic
- Pentatonic (major and minor)
- Pentatonic blues (blues scale)
- Pentatonic minor 6 (or penta dominant)
- Pentatonic m7b5
- Diminished or Half Diminished
- Whole Tone
- Augmented
- 9 Tone Augmented

Bonus

- 5 Bebop scales
- 8 Rare Extra Pentatonics
- 8 Rare Extra Scales

= 142 diagrams, 142 scales

How to Use Scales

Learn The Sound

The first step in learning a scale or a mode is to learn how it sounds on its own and then on a specific chord. Each scale or mode has a primary sound it is meant for, as most modern music is composed using chords accompanying the theme, working with scales and chords together is relevant.

In music, there are usually two main options when it comes to chords and key center:

- You have a sequence of chords creating a progression, and belonging to one or several key centers related to one or several scales.

- You have one static chord held for a few bars, and moving into something else (another static chord or a chord progression), sometimes you will just have a bass line, a vamp, or a bass note suggesting a key, a chord or a scale.

For each of those options you will always have a choice to use different scales and create different sounds. There is no precise rule; it largely depends on the composer and music style. I suggest that you learn each scale/mode according to a chord type.

Here are the most used scales ever, so it might be a good idea working on those first...

Maj7 Chord: Major Scale, Major Pentatonic Scale
Min7 Chord: Dorian Mode (2nd mode of Major Scale), Major/Minor Pentatonic Scale
MinMaj7: Harmonic Minor Scale
7 Chord: Mixolydian Mode (5th mode of Major Scale), Major Pentatonic Scale
7 Alt Chord: Superlocrian mode (7th mode of Minor Melodic Scale)
m7b5 Chord: Locrian mode (7th mode of Major Scale)

So by knowing how to use the major scale and some relative modes, the major pentatonic scale (and its minor relative), the minor melodic scale, along with the harmonic minor scale, you should know enough to play thousands of tunes!

4 scale types only open you the realm of unlimited improvisation, and with only the major scale you can already do so much! Let's see how to proceed and work with one scale. You can then apply the routine to any other type of scale.

Static Chord Workout

Now record a track of your own or use the playbacks you can download for free from www.encyclopediaofscales.com with only one chord type and work on only one scale in one key first. For example, have a track with a **Cmaj7** chord (**CEGB**) looping for 5 minutes and start playing the **C** major scale over it. You want to start from the note **C**, play a bunch of different notes, try to create a melody and go back to **C**. Then do the same by starting on the next note of the chord: **E**, then **G** and last **B**. If you don't know how to get started, try to play only half notes first, then only quarter notes, then try to mix and add silence.

Try to use only 2 or 3 notes of the scale at first and create music out of it, then add up more notes. You can play with intervals such as **123**, **156** and so on. Once you feel comfortable with **Cmajor** over **Cmaj7**, change your playback to another key; **GMaj7** for example and start all over. Continue moving from one key to another until you have played in all 12 keys. This is a big amount of work; don't feel overwhelmed there is no hurry! You can work on **1 key** for **1 week** and then switch to another key the week after. You first steps are the most important ones; if you go too fast you will stumble sooner.

If you look at the chord types listed above you will see that you will be using 4 modes of the major scale (**Ionian, Dorian, Mixolydian, Locrian**) so if you know your major scales well, you're already working ahead and mastering those other modes will be much easier. By now you should know and hear the sound of a **Maj7** chord and the major scale. You can go on and move to another chord type and start again with the same routine, or you can keep working on the same scale and work on chord progressions as explained below.

Chord Progression workout

There is a wide variety of possible chord progressions, we are going to cover the most common type, the ii V I in major and minor keys, as this chord sequence is found in thousands of tunes, it is a good idea to practice, and learn how to play over it.

What is a ii V I?

We use roman numbers for chord analysis, let's take the major scale. It is composed of 7 notes, which give us 7 chords and modes (check out the major scale page for details), if we take the first, second and fifth degree and write down their respective chord we get:

Second degree is a minor 7 chord, the fifth degree is a 7 chord and the first degree is a Maj7 chord.
From the C major scale we respectively get: **Dm7, G7, Cmaj7**
Dm7 is the **ii**, **G7** the **V7** and **Cmaj7** the **Imaj7**
In short ii V I in C = **Dm7 G7 Cmaj7**
In Bb major we get: **Fm7 C7 Bbmaj7**, and so on in all 12 keys.

The ii V i has a minor version derived from the harmonic or melodic minor scale. Let's take the ii V and i degree of a minor harmonic scale we get an m7b5 chord, a 7chord and a min chord.

In Cm we get respectively: **Dm7b5, G7, Cm (Maj7)**
In short a minor ii V i in C = **Dm7b5, G7 Cmin**
in Ab minor we get: **Bbm7b5 Eb7 Abmin**

Tension/Resolution

It is a very important concept in music, whenever we build tension there is at some point a need for resolution. Usually we would say that minor7 and major7 chords are resolution chords, whereas, the 7 chord has tension. But you can create tension over a minor7 or major7th chord and resolve it as well. You need to experiment with this.

On an ii V I, the V7 chord creates tension as it is composed of a **Tritone** (the 3rd and b7 of the chord) which is an unstable interval that needs to resolve into the I chord that follows. Thus we can build a lot of tension on the V7 chord, and add tensions to it such as a **b9**, **#9**, **b5** or **#5**. Different scales can help us make that sound pops out.

So if you look at a ii V I in terms of tension and resolution you would see:

ii = no tension
V7 = tension
I = resolution

If you like more tension, you could build tension from the beginning (the ii) and only resolve it on the I.

How to practice over ii V I?

The simplest way is to have a loop playing a ii V I in one key, is work on the major version first, so let's say you start with a loop **I Dm7 I G7 I Cmaj7 I Cmaj7 I**
As all the chords are derived from the C major scale you can use the C major scale to play on those chords. While the harmony is moving from one chord to another some notes will sound better on some chords and note so good on others.

First try to play only the root of each chord, then the third, then the fifth, and last the 7th. Then try to play the root + one other note from the scale, then the 3rd + one other note from the scale, then the 5th + one other note from the scale, then the 7th + one other note from the scale, and repeat this again but with 2 extra notes.
Now try to play the 3rd of the first chord, and the fifth of the second chord, basically keep mixing your starting notes. Once you feel comfortable move to another key.
If you play **F** on **Dm7** and **G7** it will sound great, but not as great on **Cmaj7,** as the **F** is going to rub against the **E** which is the major 3rd of **Cmaj7**. Creating music is like cooking, you need to experiment and work a lot before you get a good recipe!

The idea is to really work hard to create melodies using only the major scale, you can then move forward and repeat the same workout over a minor ii V I.

Patterns

Patterns are to music what workout is to the human body, do 200 push-ups a day you will be good at push-ups, not necessarily good at fighting, but if you spend 30 minutes boxing instead, you may become a good fighter eventually. Spending hours on patterns, will make you good at playing patterns that everybody will recognize. Of course patterns are part of music, just be careful as how you use them, and try spending your time creating melodies or lines rather than exercises.

It is very easy to create patterns, just use numbers; once again for the purpose of a clear explanation we'll use the C major scale. We label each note accordingly to its interval name:

C:1 D:2 E:3 F:4 G:5 A:6 B:7

Usually after the first few cells you understand and hear where the pattern is meant to go

Now let's start with the math! Here are a few common sequences you could work on for any scale you choose:

123 234 345 456 567 = CDE EFG FGA GAB
1234 2345 3456 4567 5678
1324 3546 5768
135 246 357 468
1357 2468 3579 46810

Play those in quarter notes, triplet and so on. Of course you can also descend:
7654 6543 5432 4321

Try to write your own patterns, this will give you some originality Try to work on a scale and create your own lines not necessarily using patterns, and whenever you catch something great, write it down or record it!

Shake and Mix

Possibilities are endless, the good choice is the choice you hear, the notes you like. With time some scales will become more familiar and friendly to your ears and you will enjoy them more, find a way to use them. It takes time.

Let's discuss some more advanced options. Re-use the same playback as before.

On a C Maj7 static chord:

- Play the C major scale, then the **C Lydian** mode (G major scale), then the C lydian augmented mode (A melodic minor).
- Now try to play on a ii V I, and when you hit the Cmaj7 play any of those 3 scales and try to make it sound nice. On a ii V I, try to play the V7 as an altered chord.
- Play C major scale on the Dm7, and Cmaj7, but when you hit the G7, play the **G Superlocrian** mode (Ab melodic minor).

On a Cmin7 static chord:

- Play C minor pentatonic, then D minor pentatonic, then G minor pentatonic. Play **D Dorian** scale (Cmajor), then D melodic minor, switch between any of those.
- Then play the C half diminished scale for 1 or 2 bars and come back to C Dorian.
- Try to fit an uncommon scale for 4 bars: harmonic minor, double harmonic minor or augmented scale starting on the **b3** (**Eb**), then back to C Dorian.

On a ii V I minor:

Try to play the ii V as a big **V7b9b13**, using the **Mixlydian b9 b13** mode over the 2 bars and then resolve it to a melodic minor, or **Aeolian** mode on the I.

Ex in Cm: I Dm7b5 I G7b9b13 I Cm I Cm I

play **G Mixolydian b9 b13** mode (=C minor harmonic) over both I Dm7b5 I G7b9b13 I;
And when you hit the Cm, play C melodic minor.

There are many more options, using the **Chord Scale Relationship Appendix** you can experiment more and more, and eventually come out with your own favorite recipes.

You will find extra material on the DVD: including demonstrations on how to work with scales !!!

7 Note Scales

A 7 note scales is maybe the most regular scale type and has been used to compose so many popular jazz and classical melodies. Those scales give us the widest variety of sounds, and the modes derived from those scales, are very popular as well.

These notes are definitely a good starting point to study music and learn an instrument. Main chord types are derived from those scales, and even pentatonic scales are mostly included in those larger 7 note scales.

We can see them as intervallic formulas, or half-tone, tone additions.
Many authors refer to **Tetrachord** and break the scale in two parts (1st and 2nd Tetrachord).

For example, the major scale **CDEFGAB** is **1234567**, or tones **11$^{1/2}$** and **111$^{1/2}$**.
We can see it as :
Tones: **11½ 111½**
First Tetrachord: **11½**
Second Tetrachord: **111½**

The Melodic Minor scale is:
- **CDEbFGAB**
- **12b34567**

Or: **1½ 1111½**
First Tetrachord: **1½ 1**
2nd Tetrachord: **111½**

We see that the 2nd Tetrachord of the Major, and Melodic Minor scale, are identical. Good news is; when you know the major scale you also know half of the melodic minor scale.

The most important scale to know first, and from top to bottom, is the major scale. Once you know your major scale (and its modes), the other scales are easier to learn as they are usually only **1 note** different from the major scale, or in the case of the Pentatonics; already included in the major scale.

The Major Scale

1234567

Ex: **CDEFGAB**

The most famous scale of all and these are the 7 modes derived from it.

Chord:	Mode:	Formula:
CMaj7	C Ionian /major scale : CDEFGAB	1234567
Dm7	D Dorian: DEFGABC	12b3456b7
Em7	E Phrygian: EFGABCD	1b2b345b6b7
Fmaj7#11	F Lydian: FGABCDE	123#4567
G7	G Mixolydian: GABCDEF	123465b7
Am7	A Aeolien /Natural minor scale: ABCDEFG	12b345b6b7
Bm7b5	B Locrien: BCDEFGA	1b2b34b5b6b7

So whatever mode you play you will use the exact same 7 notes **CDEFGAB**.
The topic of this book is not the study of modes, so those are just given as a quick reference.

How to read the **Tab**:
You will see a similar tab for many scales in this book; it indicates the 4 tone chord harmonization for each degree of the scale, as well as the corresponding mode name and intervallic formula, which starts on the first degree every time.

Be careful, this tab is always in **C** to make it easier to read, but if you play in another key you need to transpose!
Here is an example of the beginning of the tab transposed in **A**:

Chord:	Mode:
AMaj7	A Ionian/Major Scale: ABC#DEF#G#A
Bm7	B Dorian: BC#DEF#G#A
C#m7	C# Phrygian: C#DEF#G#A

Try to write this tab in different keys to help you learn to transpose modes.

How do modes work?

This matter is worth a full book on itself, let's keep it simple!

If we use as an example the 5th degree of the C Major Scale:
We read from the tab: **G7** chord, **G Mixolydian** mode.
Formula: **123456b7**
This means that you can play this mode over a **G7**.

For **G7**, starting from G we get those intervals:
1:G 2:A 3:B 4:C 5:D 6:E b7:F = GABCDEF

We could also think/view it differently:

When I look at this tab, I understand that any 5th degree of a major scale is a 7th Chord.
So if I play the corresponding mode over a 7th chord, it will be made of the notes from the major scale, found a 5th below the chord. For example, to play over a **G7** I can play the **C** major scale starting on a **G**, also called **G Mixolydian Mode**. To play over **A7** I can play the **D** major scale starting on the 5th aka **A**, also called **A Mixolydian Mode**.

There are 2 ways to see a mode:

1. As a scale on its own. I would then use the intervallic formula to build it (Ex: **123456b7** for **Mixolydian**).
2. Or as a mode belonging to a scale and I would then just have to figure out which scale it derives from (Ex: **G Mixolydian** = **C** Major) and play the major scale from the mode's **Tonic**.

All the modes derived from the major scale are commonly used, even though the **Phrygian** and **Locrian** modes are a bit less popular. Whatever the mode played from the tab, in **C** you will always use the notes **CDEFGAB**.

On the **DVD**, you will find sound bites along with the modes and their uses, so that you can hear those specific sounds and learn how to use them.

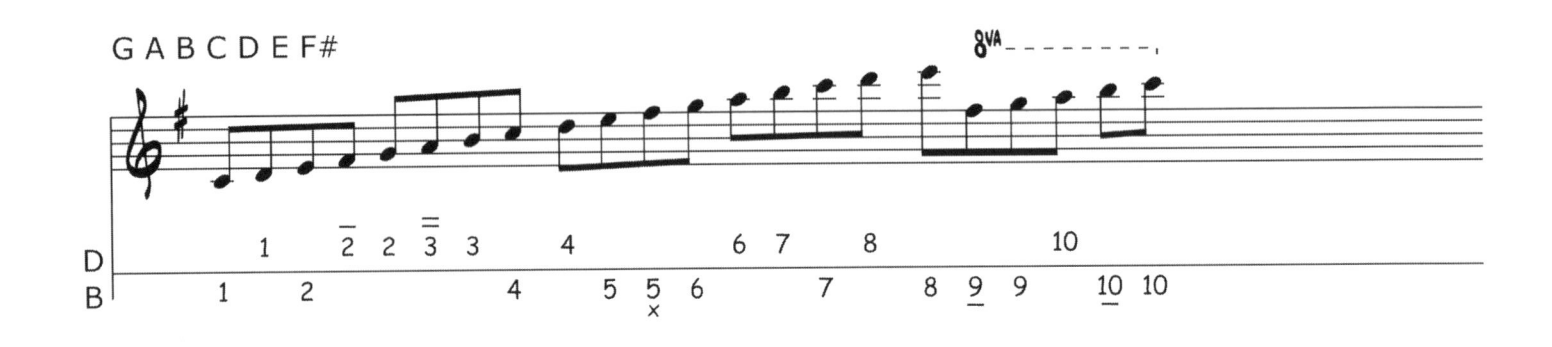

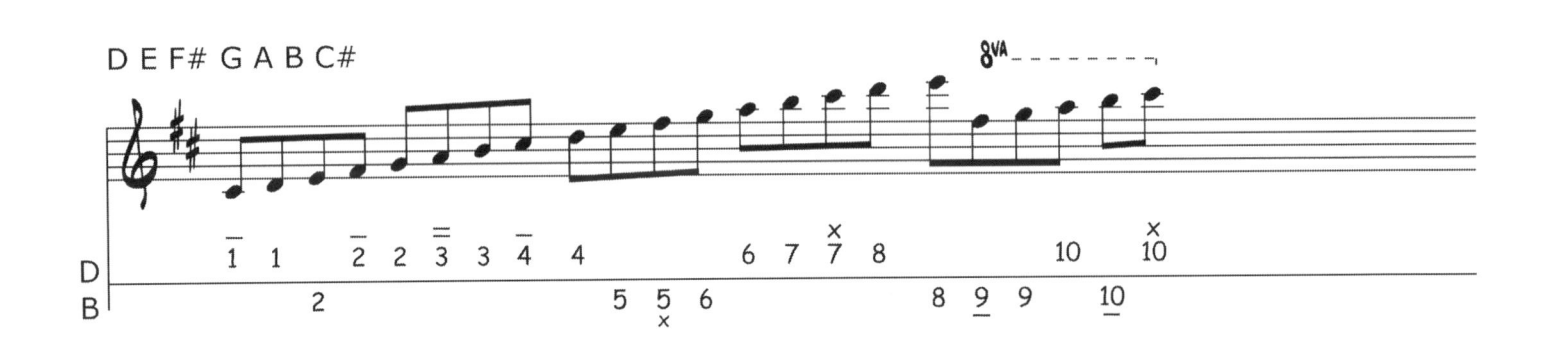

Major scale :
1234567

E F# G# A B C# D#

B C# D# E F# G# A#

F# G# A# B C# D# F

Db Eb F Gb Ab Bb C

Harmonica School ©

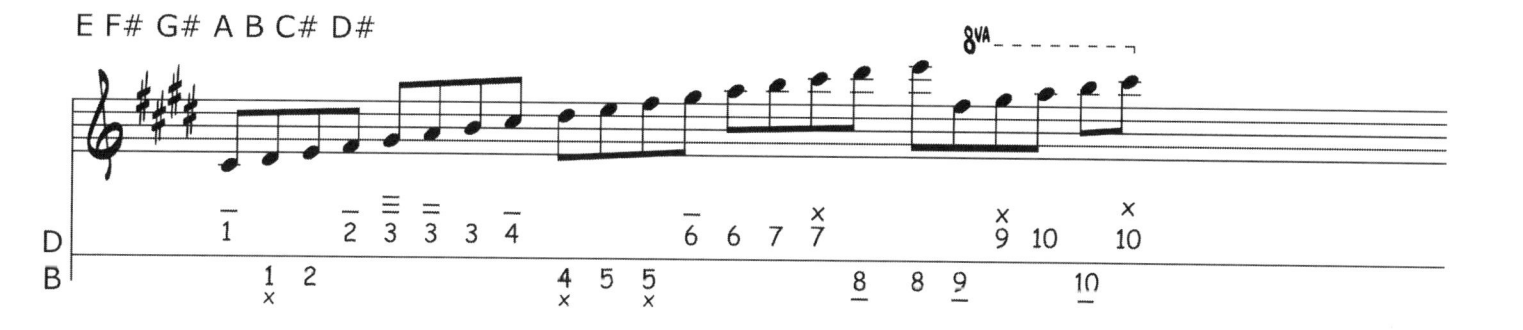

Ab-Bb-C-Db-Eb-F-G

Eb F G Ab Bb C D

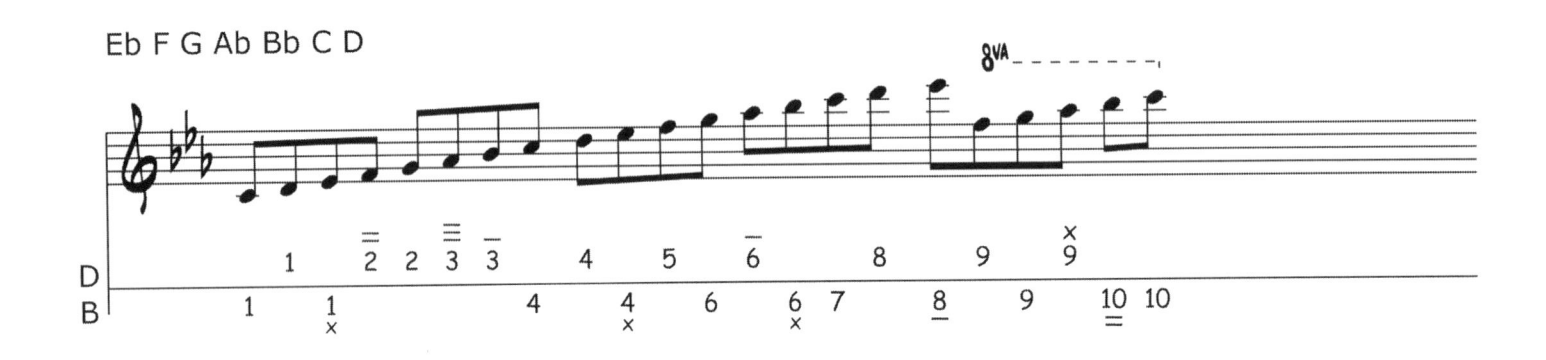

Bb C D Eb F G Ab

F G A Bb C D E F

Melodic Minor

12b34567

Ex: **CDEbFGAB**

Basically it is a major scale with a minor third. You could also see it as a **Dorian** scale with a major 7th, if you are familiar with the **Dorian** sound/mode.
But it has a very distinctive sound. As the major scale, the melodic minor scale has 7 modes, they are not all used as often as the ones found in the major scale, but some are extremely important.

Chord:	Mode:	Formula:
CmMaj7/Cm6	C Melodic Minor (Minor Jazz): CDEbFGAB	12b34567
Db9sus4	D Dorian b2: DEbFGABC	1b23456b7
EbMaj7#5	Eb Lydian #5 (Lydian Augmented): EbFGABCD	123#4#567
F7#11	F7 Lydien b7 (Bartok, Lydian dominant): FGABCDEb	123#456b7
G7b13	G Mixolydian b6 (b13): GABCDEbF	12345b6b7
Am7b5	A Locrian #2 (Aeolian b5): ABCDEbFG	12b34b5b6b7
Balt (B7#5)	B altered (Super Locrien, diminished whole tone): BCDEbFGA	1b2b33b5b6b7

The most useful modes are:
- **Minor Melodic,**
- **Altered**
- **Lydianb7**
- Lydian#5,
- Mixolydianb6,
- and Locrian #2,

The **Altered** mode, is the primarily scale used over the **Dominant Altered** chords with a V degree function, and resolving to I (Maj or Min).

For example: On **I G7#9#5 I C maj7 I**, you would play the **G Altered** mode over the **G** chord = **Ab** minor melodic.

The **Lydian** b7 mode is used over static a 7th chord or any 7#11 chord.

The scale itself is based on the chords **Cm6** (or **CEbGA**) and **G7** (or **GBDF**).

Melodic minor
1 2 b3 4 5 6 7

Harmonica school

C D Eb F G A B

Db Eb E Gb Ab Bb C

D E F G A B C#

Eb F Gb Ab Bb C D

Harmonica School ©

E F# G A B C# D#

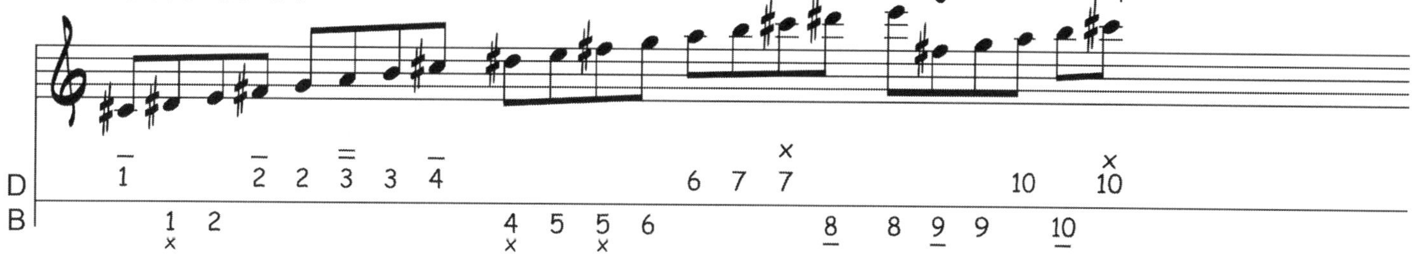

F G Ab Bb C D E

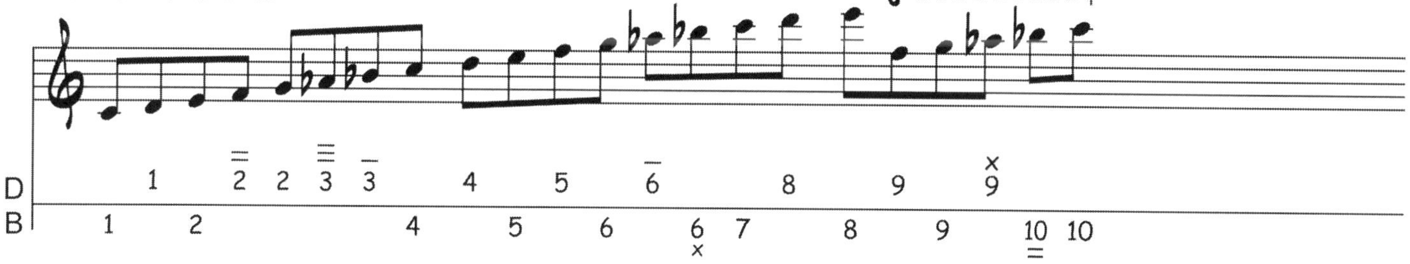

F# G# A B C# D# F

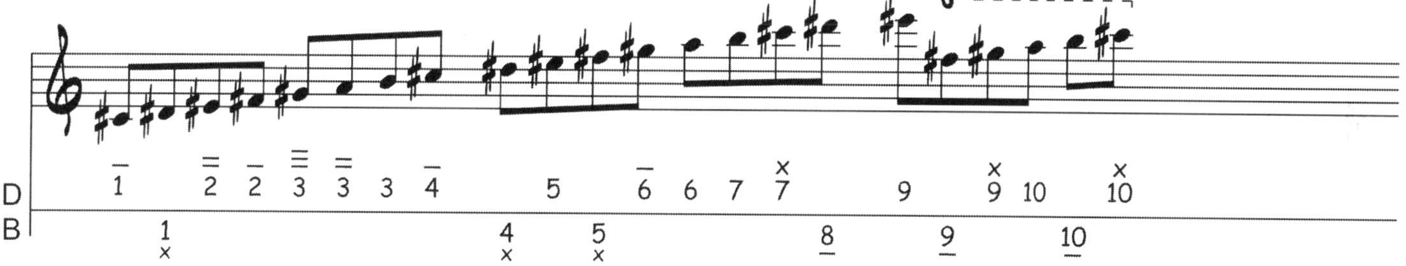

G A Bb C D E F#

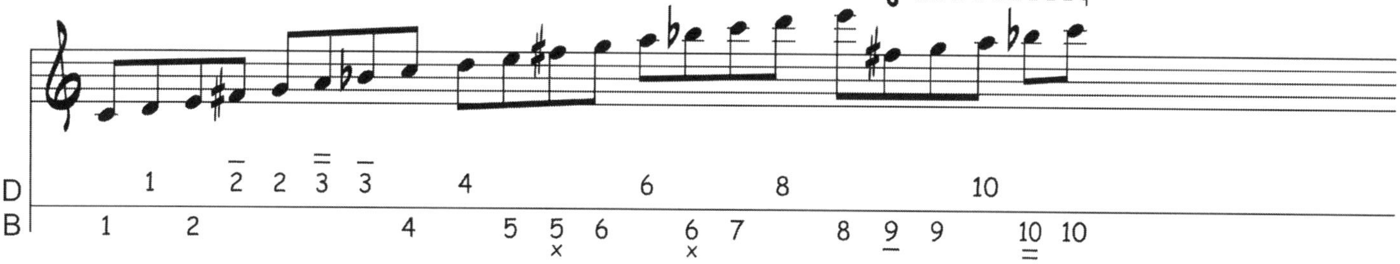

Ab Bb B Db Eb F G

A B C D E F# G#

Bb C Db Eb F G A

B C# D E F# G# A#

Harmonica School ©

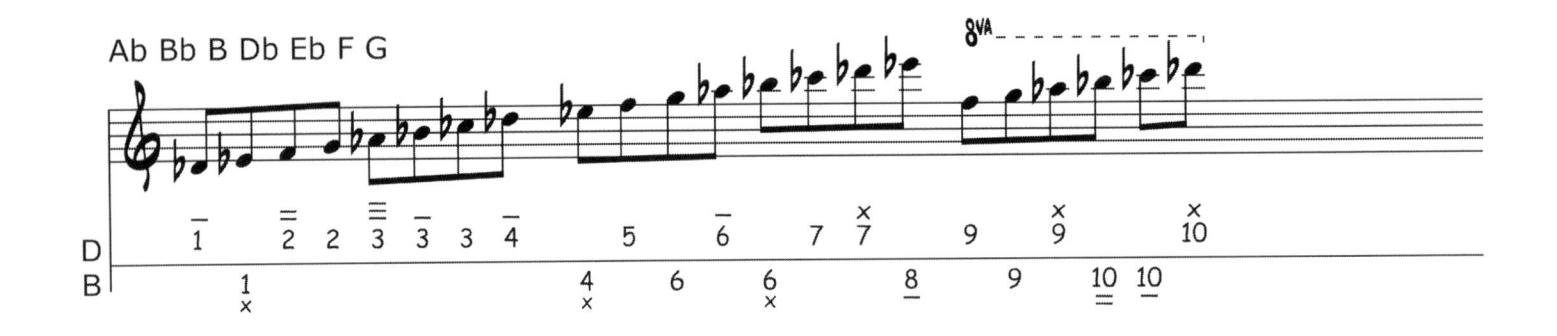

26

Harmonic minor

12b345b67

<u>Ex</u> : **CDEbFGAbB**

You can see it as a major scale with a minor third and minor 6th, or a Natural minor scale (Aeolian mode) with a major 7th.
It is an exotic scale, and some modes of this scale are used in **Traditionnal** music, and even though they all come from this harmonic minor scale, they may also be known under different names.

Like the major, and melodic minor scale, the harmonic minor scale has 7 modes:

Chord:	Mode:	Formula:
CmMaj7	Harmonic minor : CDEbFGAbB	12b345b67
Dm7b5	Locrian#6 : DEbFGAbBC	1b2b34b56b7
EbMaj7#5	Ionian augmented (Ionian#5): EbFGAbBCD	12b34#567
Fm7#11	Dorian#4 (Romanian): FGAbBCDEb	12b3#456b7
G7b9b13	Mixolydianb2b6 (phrygian dominant, Spanish Gispy, Jewish): GAbBCDEbF	1b2345b6b7
AbMaj7#9#5	Lydian#2 : AbBCDEbFG	1#23#4567
Bdim7	Diminished (ultralocrian) : BCDEbFGAb	1b2b33#4#56

The most used modes are :
Harmonic Minor, Diminished and Phrygian Dominant

The **Mixolydienb2b6** is the mode used for a 7th sub-dominant chord acting as a III7 or VII7.

I **Cmaj** I **E7b9** I **Am7** I

Here on E7b9 that acts as the III7 of C, the Mixolydianb2b6 mode is the better choice. You would play: **EFG#ABCDE = A harmonic minor scale**.

Same for dim7 chords:
I **Cmaj7** I **C#dim7** I **Dm7** I

On C#dim7 you would play the D harmonic minor scale.

Harmonic minor
1 2 b3 4 5 b6 7

E F# G A B C D#

F G Ab Bb C Db E

F# G# A B C# D F

G A Bb C D Eb F#

Harmonica School ©

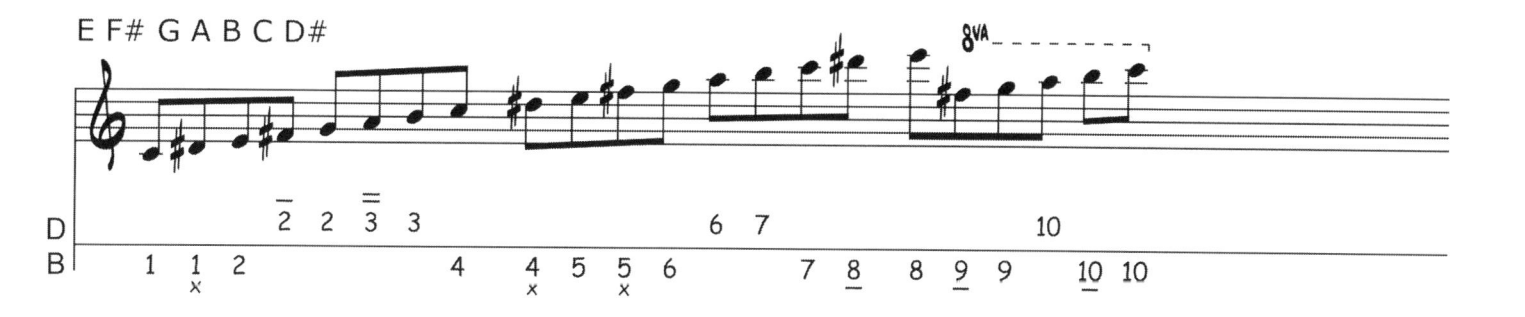

Ab Bb B Db Eb E G

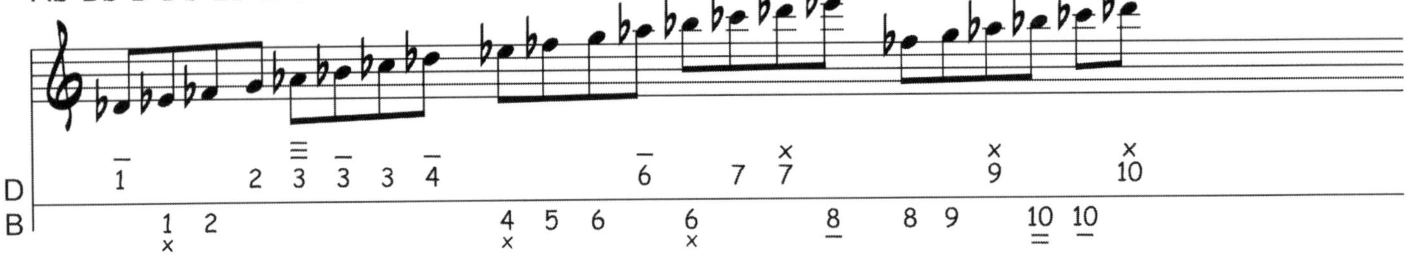

A B C D E F G#

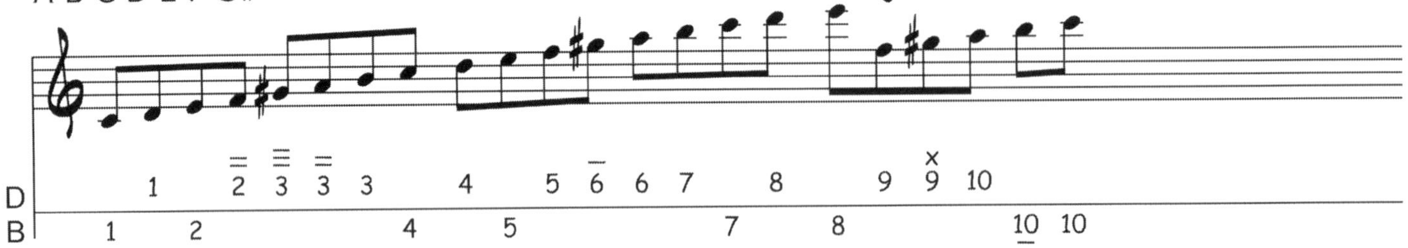

Bb C Db Eb F Gb A

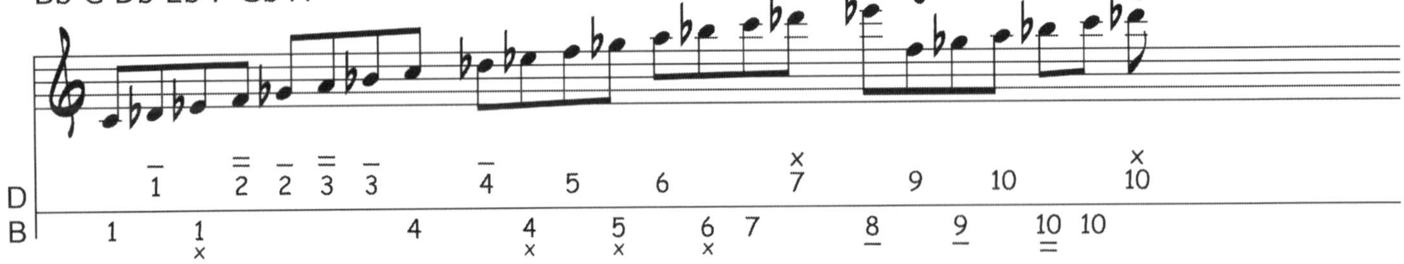

B C# D E F# G A#

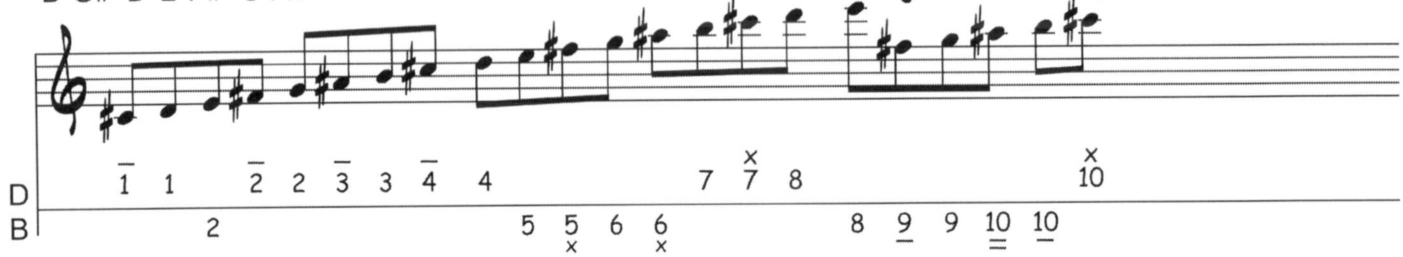

Harmonic Major

12345b67

Ex : **CDEFGAbB**
Same as a major scale but with a b6.
Same as a harmonic minor scale but with a major 3rd

Chord:	Mode:	Formula:
Cmaj7#5	Harmonic major (Ionian b6) : CDEFGAbB	12345b67
Dm9b5	Dorianb5 (Locrian#2#6) : DEFGAbBC	12b34b56b7
Em7 (Ealt)	Phrygianb4 (Superphrygian) : EFGAbBCD	1b2b335b6b7
FmMaj7	Lydianb3 : FGAbBCDE	12b3#4567
G7b9	Mixolydianb2 : GAbBCDEF	1b23456b7
Abmaj7#5	Lydian augmented#2 : AbBCDEFG	1b33b5b667
Bdim7	Locrian diminished: BCDEFGAb	1b2b34b5b66

It has a typical sound with the first mode over a Maj7#5 chord; other modes are much less used. Try the Phrygian b4 over an altered chord and the Dorian b5 over a m7, a m7b5 or even a 7#11 chord. Also try to use the harmonic major scale over a regular ii V I progression.

Harmonic Major

12345b67

E F# G# A B C D#

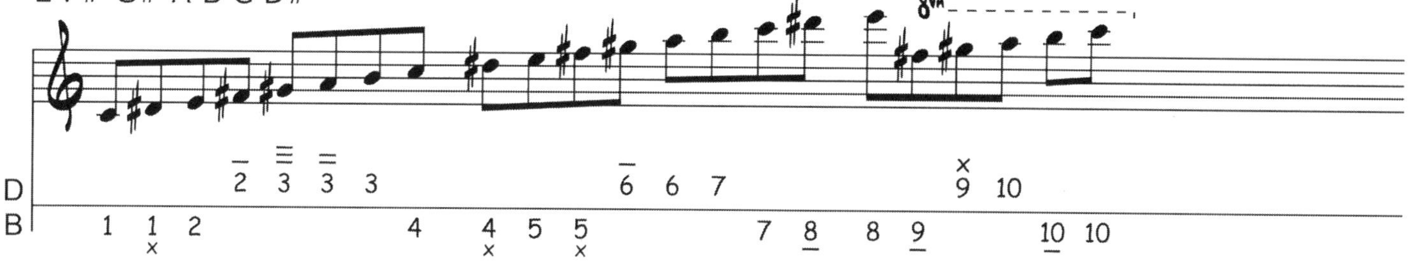

F G A Bb C Db E

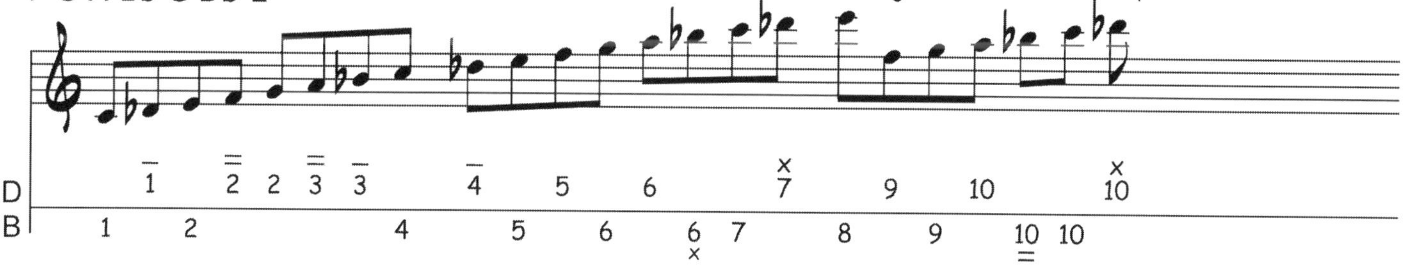

F# G# A# B C# D F

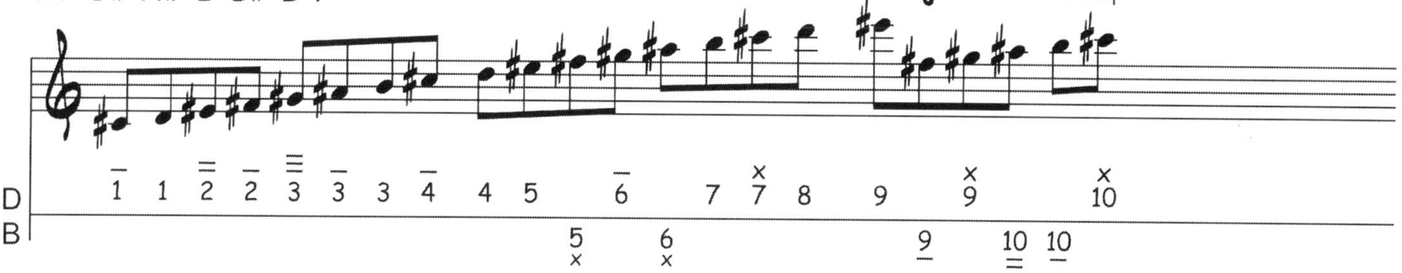

G A B C D Eb F#

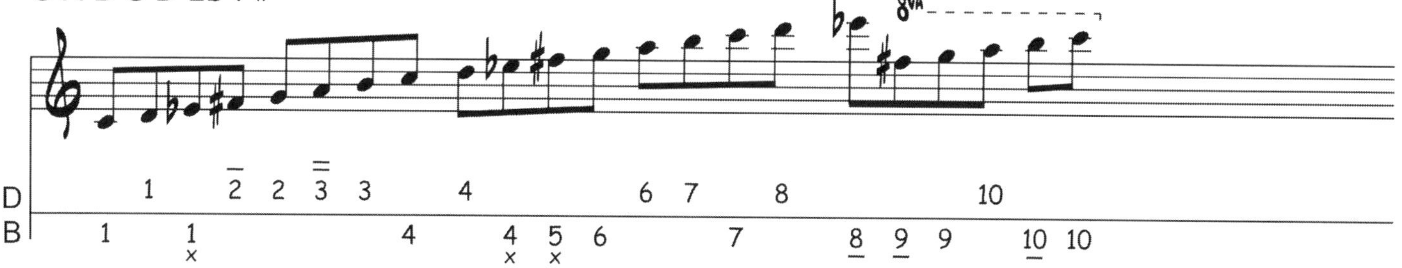

Ab Bb C Db Eb E G

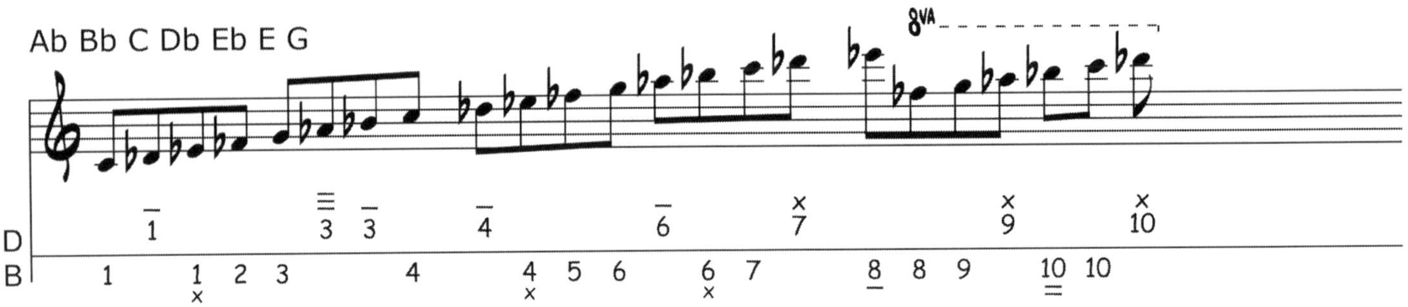

A B C# D E F G#

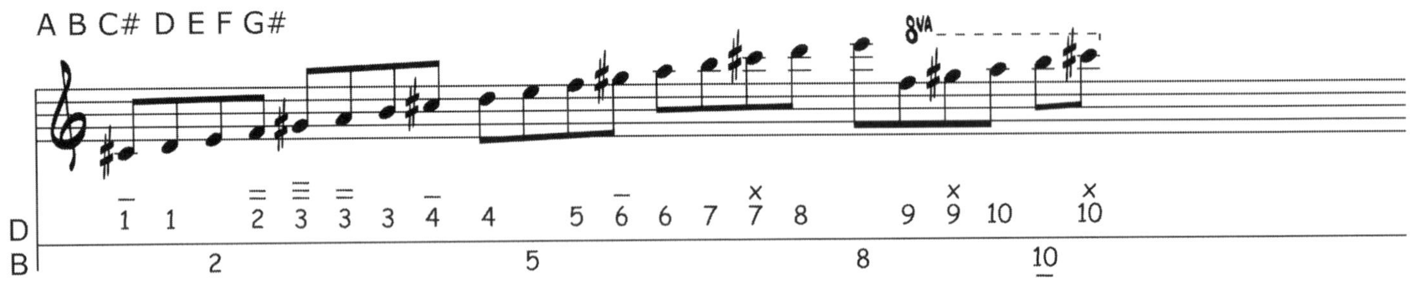

Bb C D Eb F Gb A

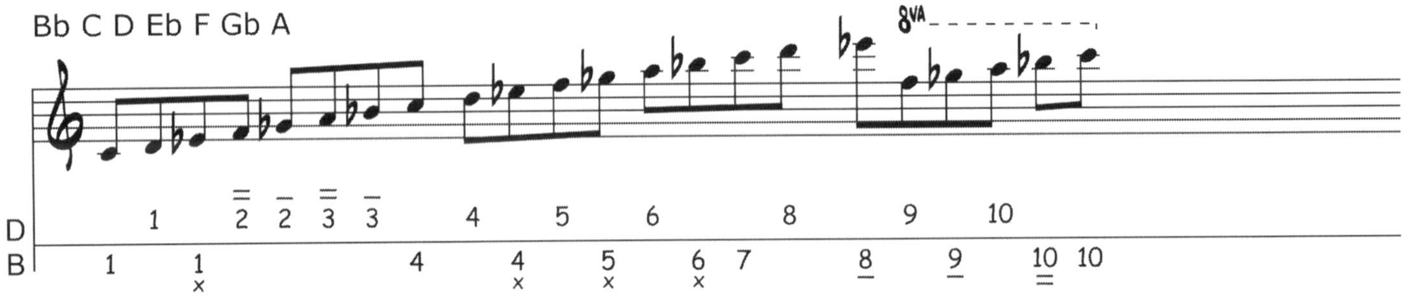

B C# D# E F# G A#

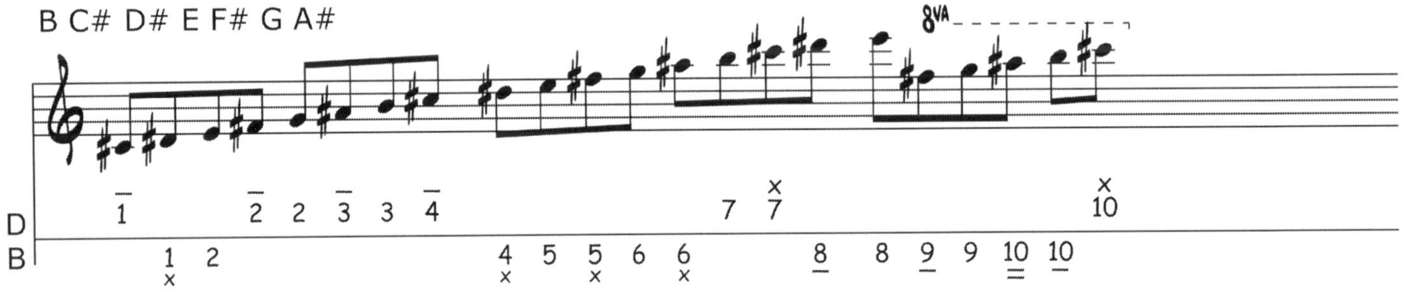

Double Harmonic Minor

12b3#45b67

Ex: **CDEbF#GAbB**

The Double Harmonic Minor Scale is also called the **Byzantine Scale**, the **Hungarian Gypsy Scale** or the **Gypsy Scale**.
As with the other 7 note scales, this scale has 7 modes but only 3 are mainly used. Having a closer look at the scale harmonization sheds more info on why:
Most chords get dissonant tensions added, which make the mode hard to use. For example, the 3rd mode has a perfect 4th and #4 to play over a Maj7 chord, the #4 is a better choice but, we almost never use both at the same time. We also get a very tough minor 3rd (A very rough sound over a Maj7 chord), which you can of course still experiment with.
Here are the frequently used modes:
1. The 1st mode Double Harmonic Minor (**CDEbF#GAbB**)
2. The 2nd mode called Oriental Scale.

This scale is a good example of what you could find in several books referenced as **Exotic Scales**, they do sound '**Exotic**' but they are not new! They all come from the same **Double Harmonic Minor Scale**.
Oriental Scale: **CDbEFGbABb**
Double Harmonic Minor Bb: **BbCDbEFGbA**
And the 5th mode, also found under the name **Double Major Harmonic**, is again the very same scale.

Double Harmonic Major: 1b2345b67
Ex: C **Double Harmonic Major** = **CDbEFGAbB**
    = F **Double Harmonic Minor**: **FGAbBCDbE**

Chord:	Mode:	Formula:
CmMaj7	CDEbF#GAbB (Double Minor Harmonic)	12b3#45b67
D7#11	DEbF#GAbBC (Oriental)	1b234b56b7
EbMaj7#11	EbF#GAbBCD	1b334b66b7
Ab/F#	F#GAbBCDEb	1b224b5b66
GMaj7	GAbBCDEbF# (Double Major Harmonic)	1b2345b67
Ab7	AbBCDEbF#G	1b33b55b77
Bm6	BCDEbF#GAb	1b2b345b66

Recap: For the Double Harmonic Minor Scale we will use mainly the 1st, 2nd and 5th mode.

Double Harmonic Minor
1 2 b3 #4 5 b6 7

Harmonica school

C D Eb F# G Ab B

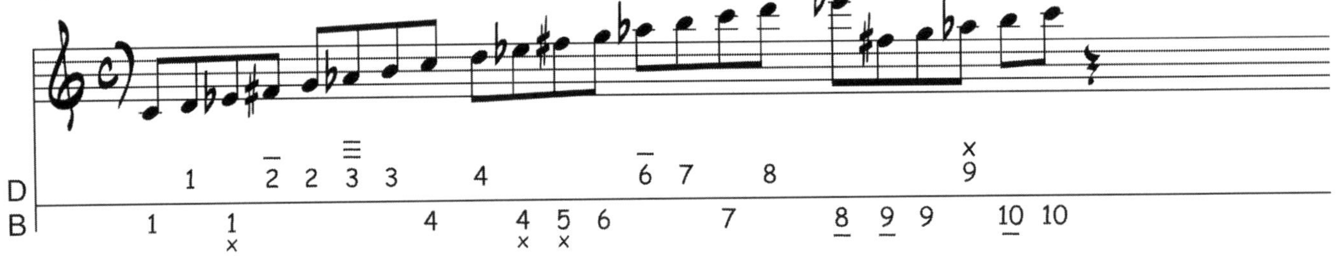

C# D# E G G# A C

D E F G# A Bb C#

Eb F Gb A Bb B D

Harmonica School ©

E F# G A# B C D#

F G Ab B C Db E

F# G# A C C# D F

G A Bb C# D Eb F#

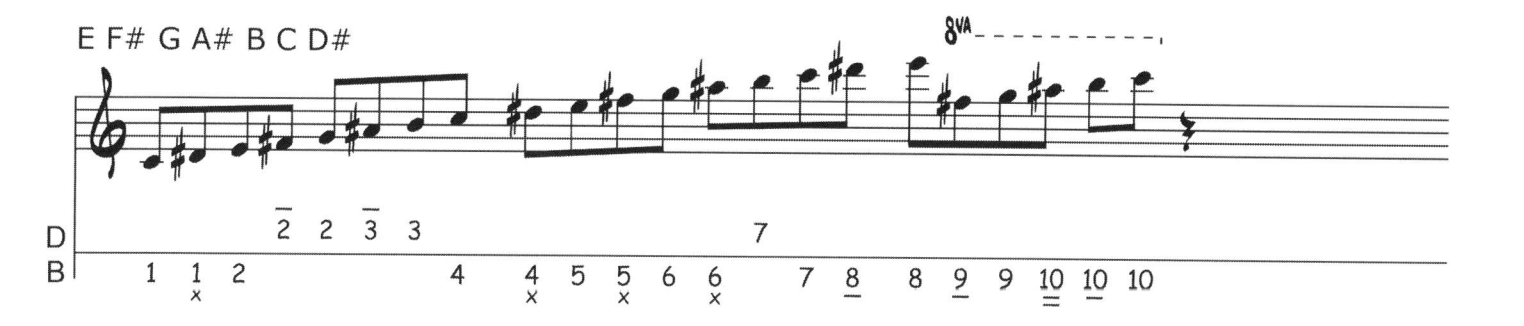

Harmonica School ©

G# A# B D D# E G

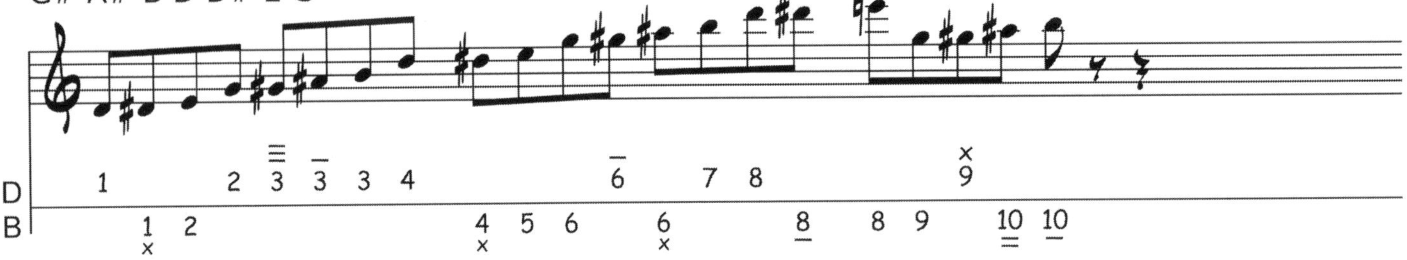

A B C D# E F G#

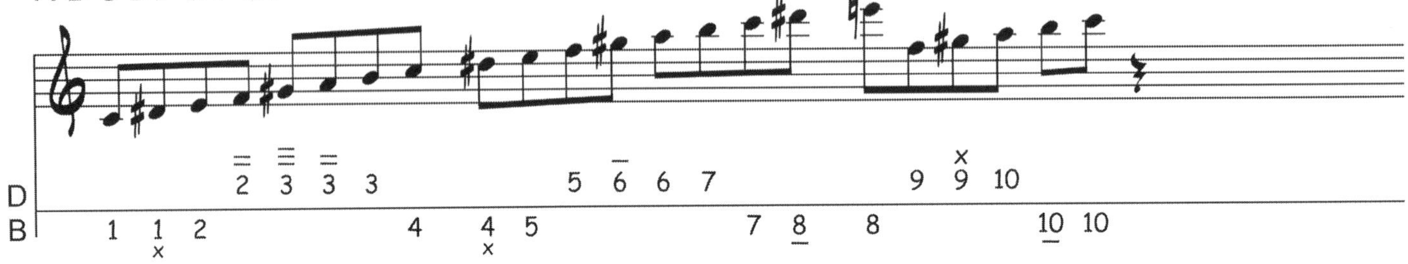

Bb C Db E F Gb A

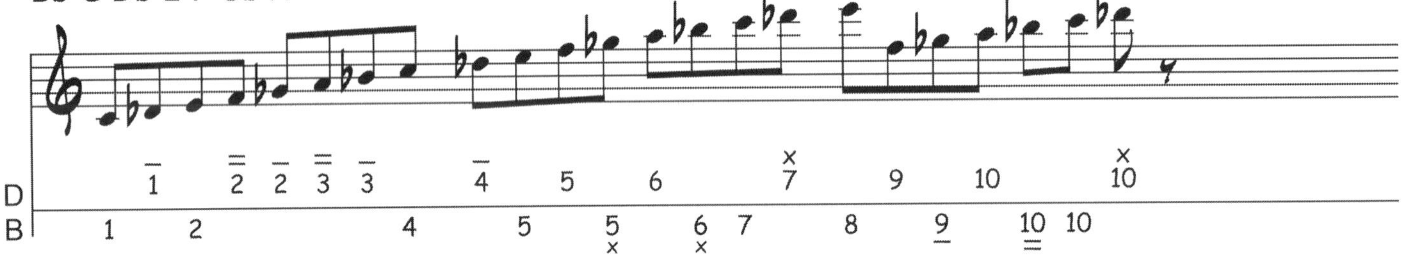

B C# D F F# G A#

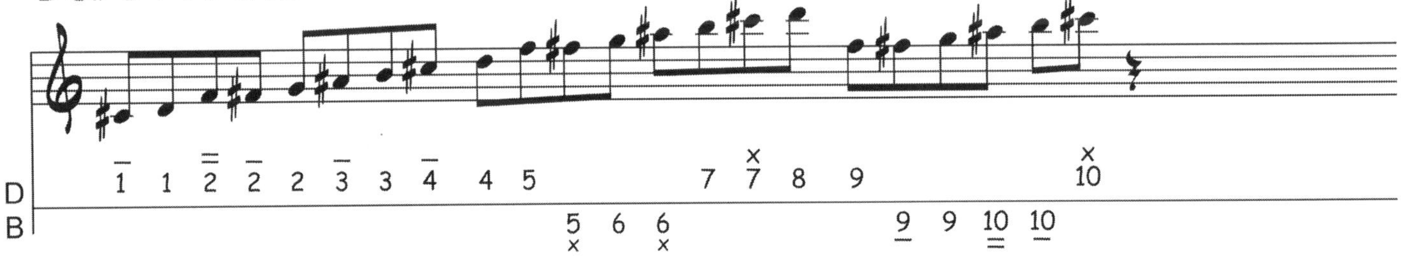

Pentatonic Scales

Pentatonic Scales are 5 note scales, including the **Blues** scale, which has six notes, because it is really just a **Pentatonic** scale with an extra passing tone, and can for this reason be used in the exact same way as the **Regular Pentatonic**.

Pentatonic scales are almost always part of another larger scale. For example, the Major/ Minor Pentatonic, the Dominant Pentatonic (minor 6) and the m7b5 Pentatonic, are all included in the major scale!

They have an **Arpeggio** like character to them (most **Arpeggios** are 4 or 5 notes long), and usually use a stack of 4th in their structure which give them an edgy modern sound.

For example:
A **Minor Pentatonic** (C major) can be seen as a stack of 4th starting on E: **EADGC**. Using those 4th intervals make them sound really modern. Finally, as they are light structures you can more easily combine them, or switch from one to another, in order to create inside or outside harmonic movement.

For example:
On a **Cmaj7#11** or **Am9**, try combining a **C** and **D Major Pentatonic**.
On a **Dm7** play **F major pentatonic** then **F# major pentatonic** to create tension and get an outside sound and then go back to **F** to resolve.

Pentatonic Scale

Major/Minor
12356/1b345b7

<u>Ex</u>: **CDEGA, CEbFGBb**

One of the most used scales in music, from **Traditional** music, to **Classic** and **Jazz**, often referred to as **Major** or **Minor Pentatonic**, but in reality these two scales are just one!

CDEGA = ACDEG

C Major Pentatonic = A Minor Pentatonic

When you learn them, just learn both sounds:

A **Minor Pentatonic** is a mode of the **C Major Pentatonic**, so instead of learning 24 scales only learn 12!

Of course both modes have a different sound, the **Major Pentatonic** is the scale over-used in **Country** music, and the **Minor Pentatonic** is the scale over-used in **Blues** and **Rock**. I'm sure you are already familiar with those sounds.

Those scales originate from **Asia**, so you will find them in **Traditional** music as well, but there is more to it!

Jazz players and **Classical** composer have used the **Pentatonic Scale** extensively

You can use the **C Major Pentatonic** over a lot of chords. Here are the most common ones:

Cmaj7, C7, Dm7, D11, Em7b5, E7b9b13, Fmaj7, F#alt, F#m7b5, Gm7, G11, Am7, A7alt, BbMaj7#11, Bm7b5 and **B7b9b13**

Pentatonic Maj / Min
12356 / 1b345b7

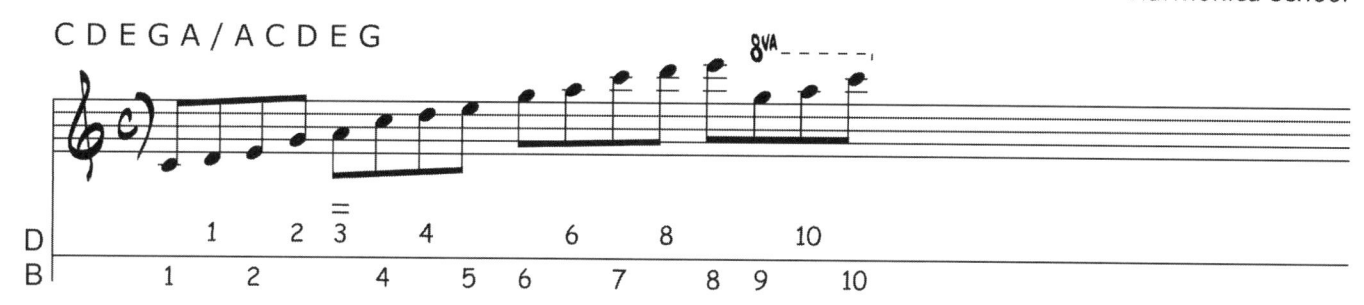

Harmonica school

C D E G A / A C D E G

Db Eb F Ab Bb / Bb Db Eb F Ab

D E F# A B / B D E F# A

Eb F G Bb C / C Eb F G Bb

Harmonica School ©

E F# G# B C# / C# E F# G# B

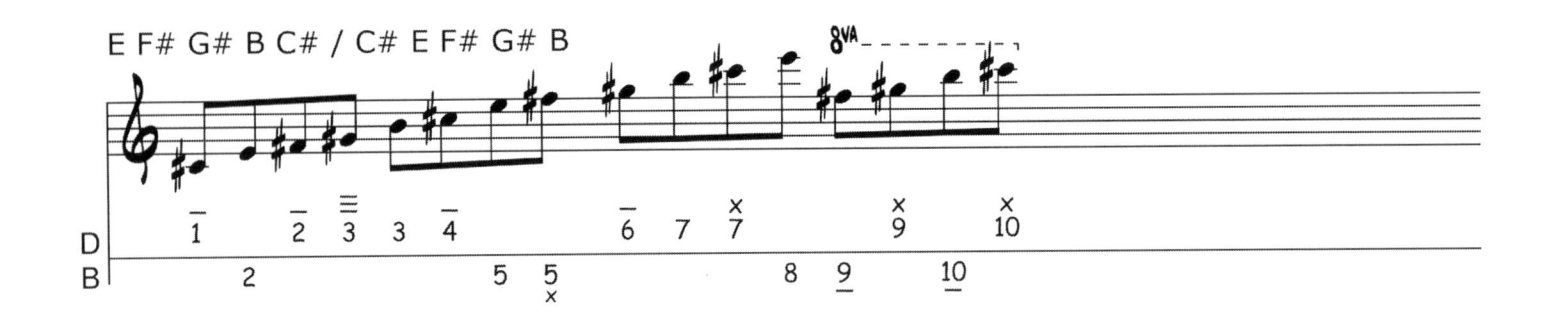

F G A C F / D F G A C

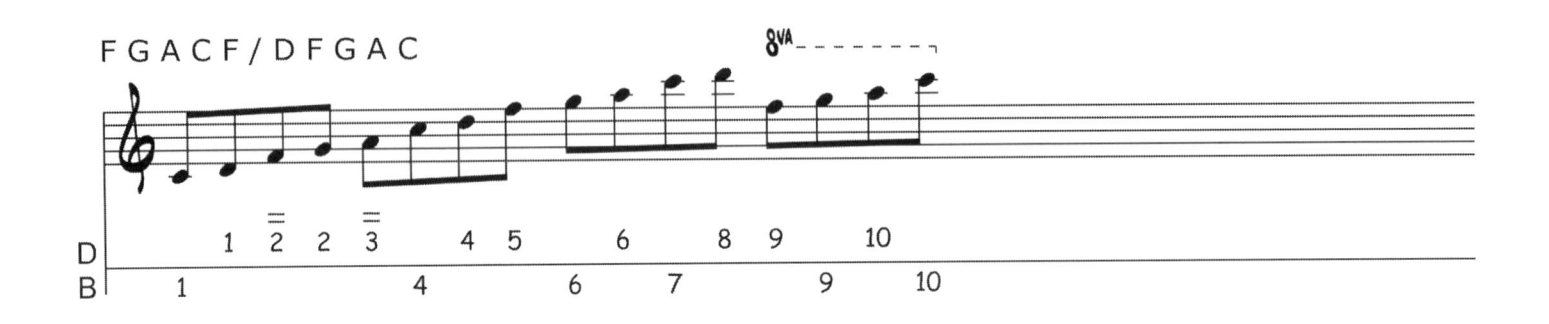

F# G# A# C# D# / D# F# G# A# C#

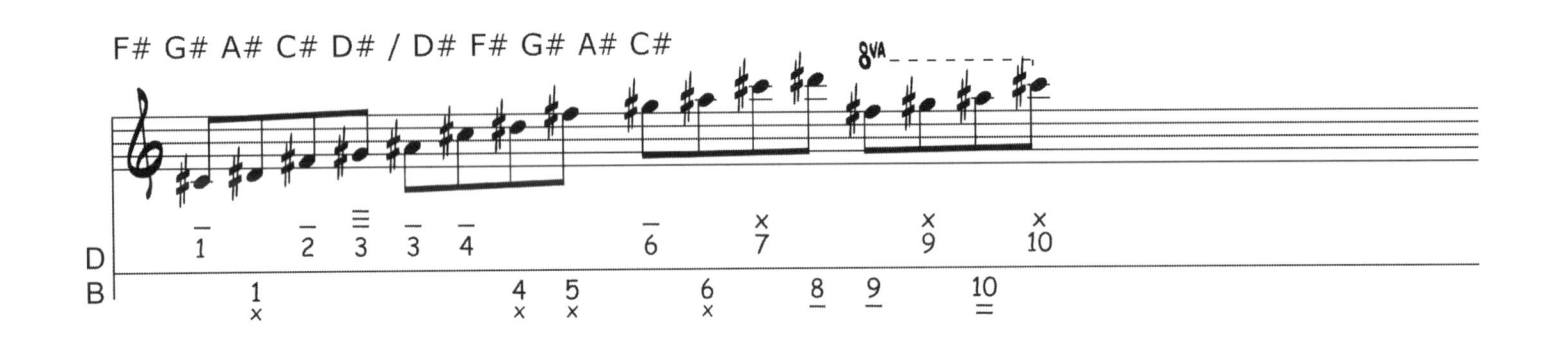

G A B D E / E G A B D

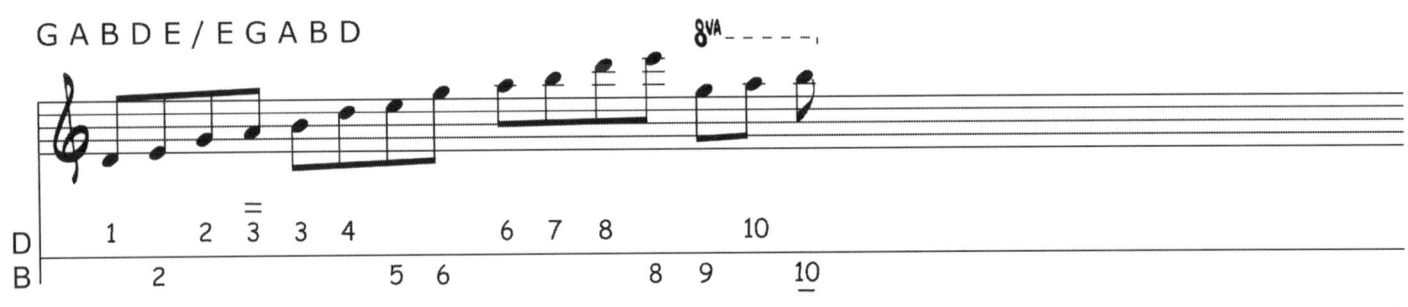

Harmonica School ©

42

Ab Bb C Eb F / F Ab Bb C Eb

A B C# E F# / F# A B C# E

Bb C D F G / G Bb C D F

B C# D# F# G# / G# B C# D# F#

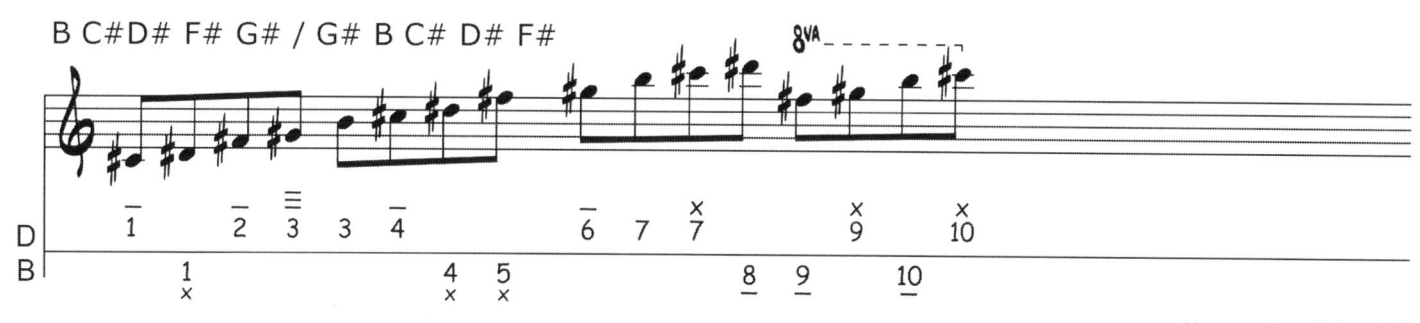

Harmonica School ©

43

Blues Scale

Major/Minor
12b3356/1b34#45b7

Ex: **CDEbEGA, CEbFF#GBb**

It is the same as a pentatonic scale with an extra "blue" note added to spice it up !

CDEbEGA = ACDEbEG

C Major blues = A Minor blues

You can use it as a regular pentatonic scale. Just experiment playing with the extra note and learn how to make it sound right. You can apply it on the same chords as the pentatonic scale.
The major blues scale has the typical sound found in jazz and country music over dominant or major chords.
The minor blues scale is the one used in blues and rock over dominant or m7 chords.

Pentatonic blues Maj / Min
12b3356 / 1b34#45b7

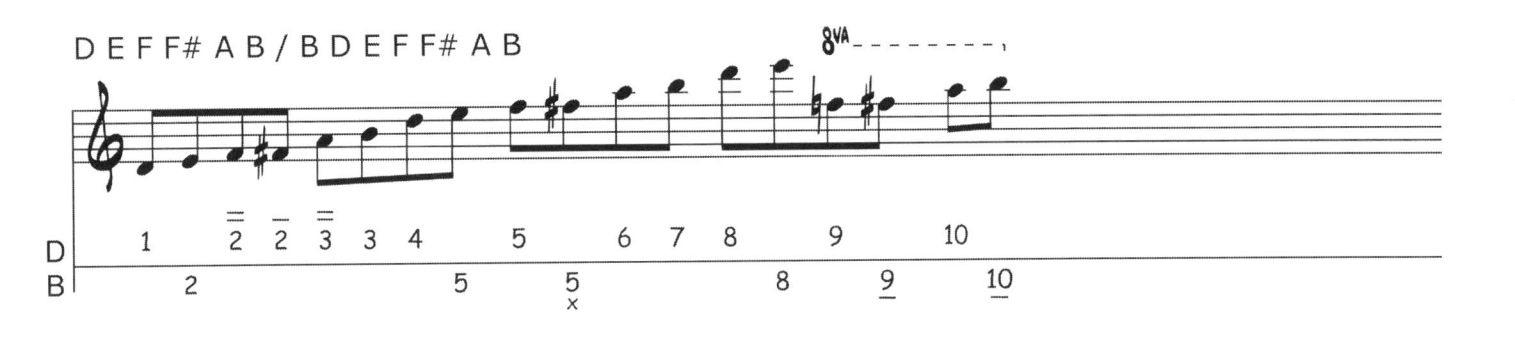

E F# G G# B C# / C# E F# G G# B

F G Ab A C D / D F G Ab A C

F# G# A A# C# D# / D# F# G# A A# C#

G A Bb B D E / E G A Bb B D

Ab Bb B C Eb F / F Ab Bb B C Eb

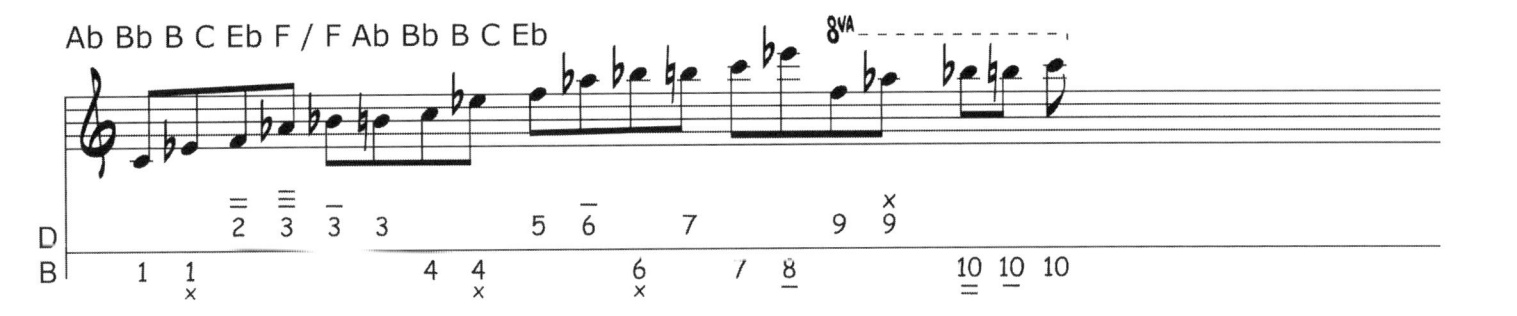

A B C C# E F# / F# A B C C# E

Bb C Db D F G / G Bb C Db D F

B C# D D# E F# G# / G# B C# D D# F#

m7b5 Pentatonic

1b34b5b7

Ex: **CEbFGbBb**

You can see it in a lot of different ways, and it's a very versatile scale.

First of all you can see it as a derivation from the **Blues Scale**: **CEbFGbGBb** minus the note **G**.

You can also see it as an **m7b5 Arpeggio** with an extra 4th: **CEbGbBb+F**

And lastly, it has been used very often as a mode of a minor scale, sometimes called **Japanese Scale**:

Hence in **Eb** (same notes starting from **Eb**): **EbFGbBbC** = **12b356** = A very exotic sound over a minor 7th chord. It has been used as such by **Sonny Rollins** and **John Coltrane**.

Usage:

Well I would suggest using, and thinking about it as, an **m7b5 Enhanced Arpeggio.**
Use the **Cm7b5 Pentatonic Scale** on: **Cm7b5**, **Ebm6**, **Ab13**, **Dalt**, and **F#Maj7#11**.

Pentatonic m7b5

1b34b5b7

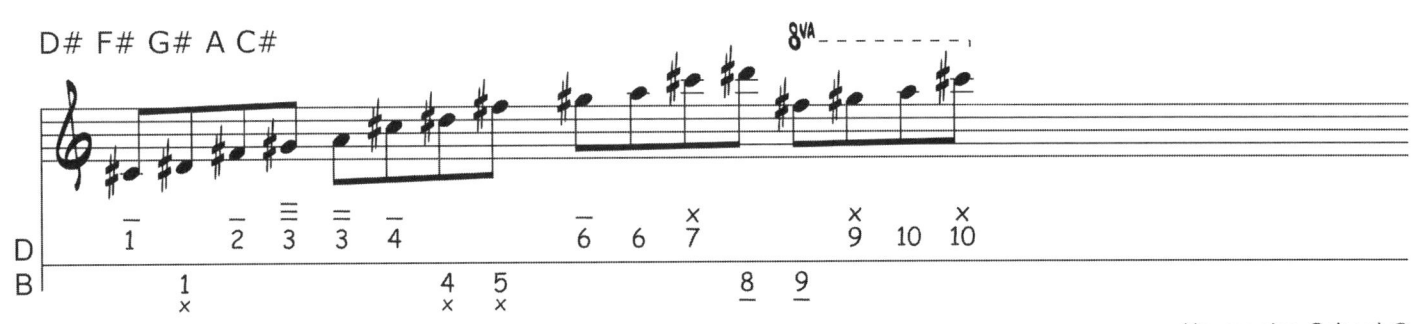

Harmonica School ©

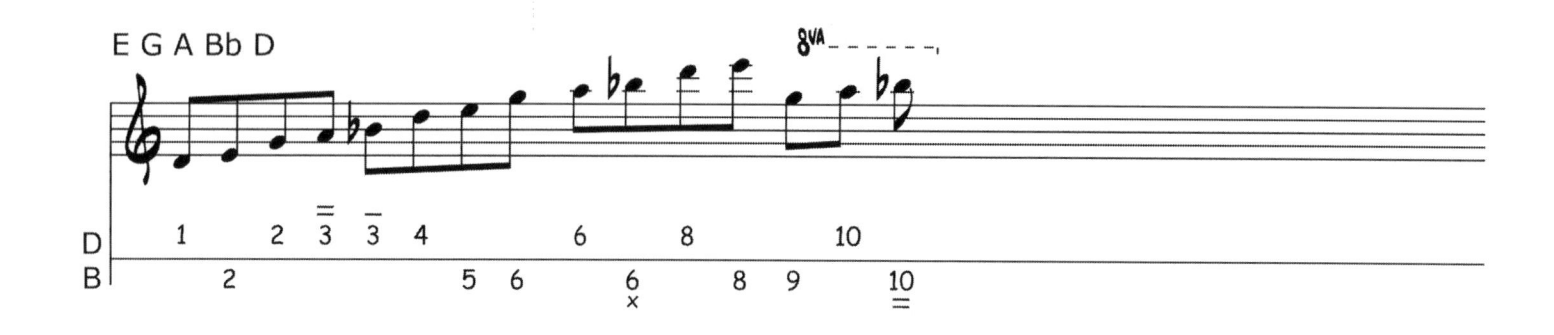

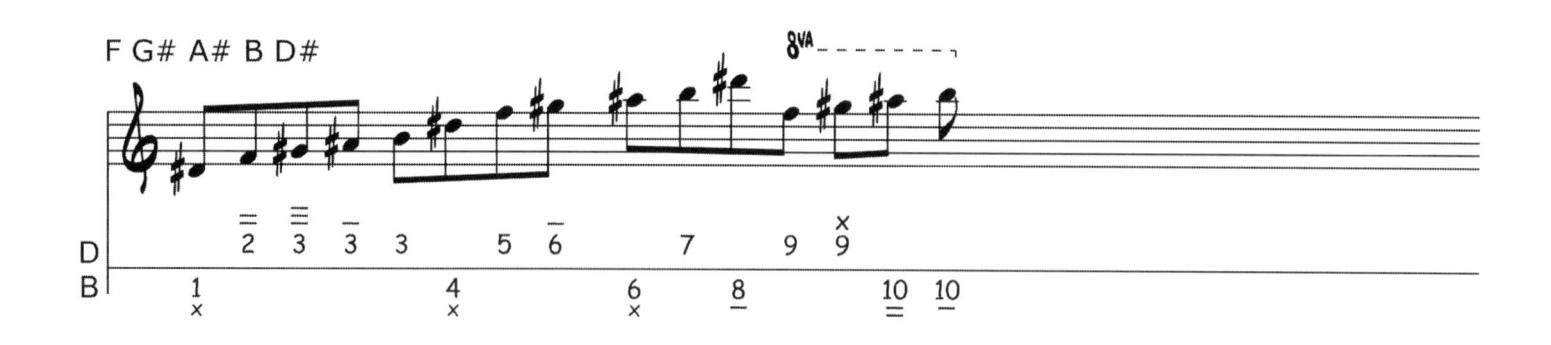

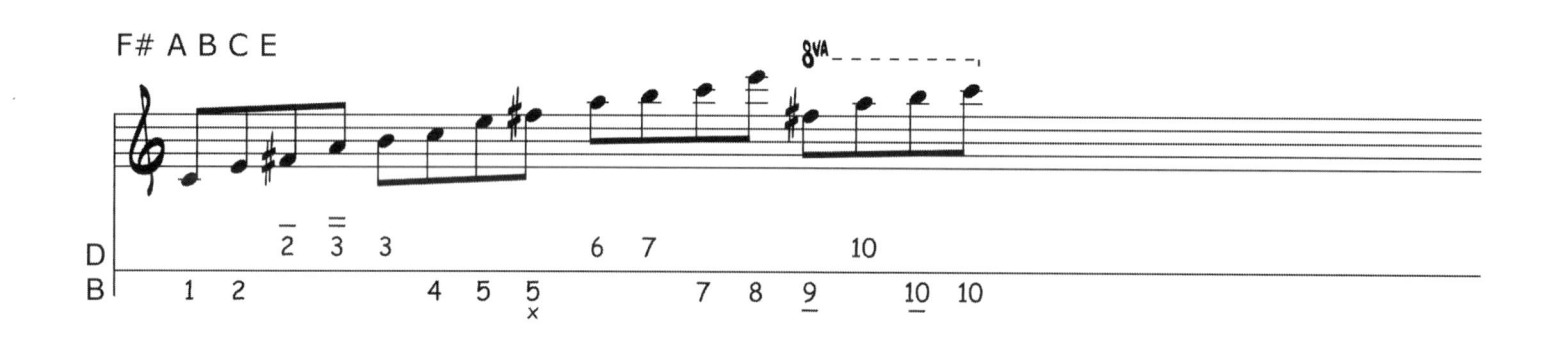

G# B C# D F#

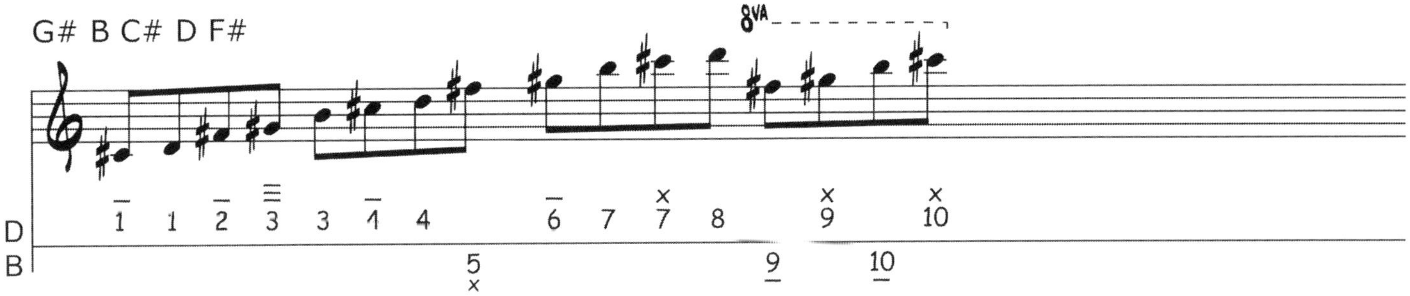

A C D Eb G

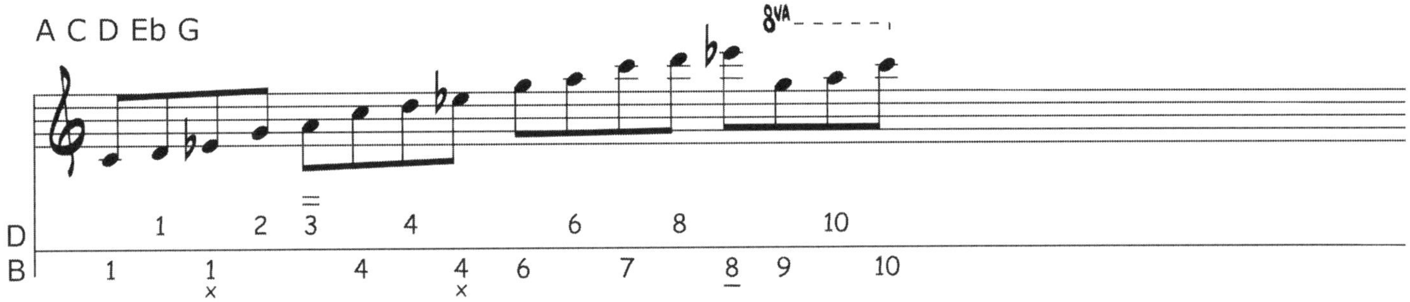

A# C# D# E G#

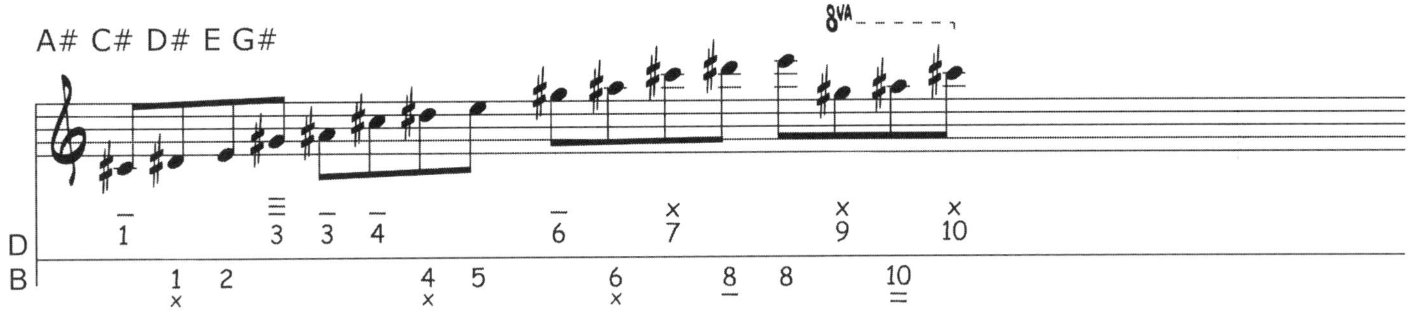

B D E F A

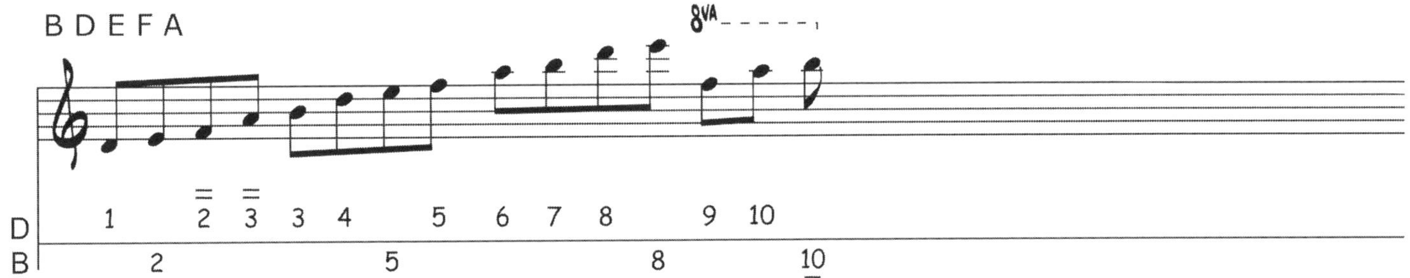

Dominant / Minor 6 Pentatonic

1235b7 / 1b3456

Ex: C Dominant: **CDEGBb**
C minor 6: **CEbFGA**

Like the major / minor pentatonic scale this dominant / minor 6 has a double basic sound

C dominant CDEGBb = Gminor6 GBbCDE

C9 = Gm6

To play a minor 6 or 7 chord starting on the 5th of a dominant 7th chord is a very common sound used by jazz musicians.

So whenever you learn this scale you should learn both the dominant and minor 6 sound.

You can see this scale as a **dominant 9th arpeggio CEGBb +D**
or a **minor pentatonic scale with a 6** instead of a b7 : **GBbCD + E**

The minor 6 sound is very interesting and gives us a pentatonic we can substitute to the melodic minor scale even though this scale can also be found in the major scale (Dm6 : DFGAB is included in C major and D melodic minor)

Usage:

Well I would suggest using **C dominant scale (Gmin6) over :**
C7, D9b13, Ealt, F#alt, Gm6/Gm7, Abmaj7#11, Am7b5, BbMaj7#11 and Bb7#11.

Dominant Pentatonic / Minor 6
1235b7 / 1b3456

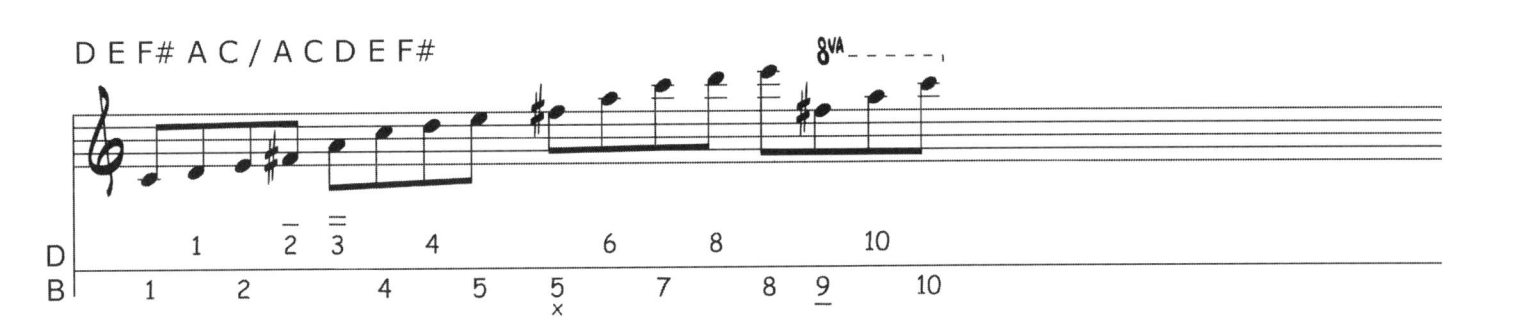

C D E G Bb / G Bb C D E

Db Eb F Ab B / Ab B Db Eb F

D E F# A C / A C D E F#

Eb F G Bb Db / Bb Db Eb F G

Harmonica School ©

53

E F# G# B D / B D E F# G#

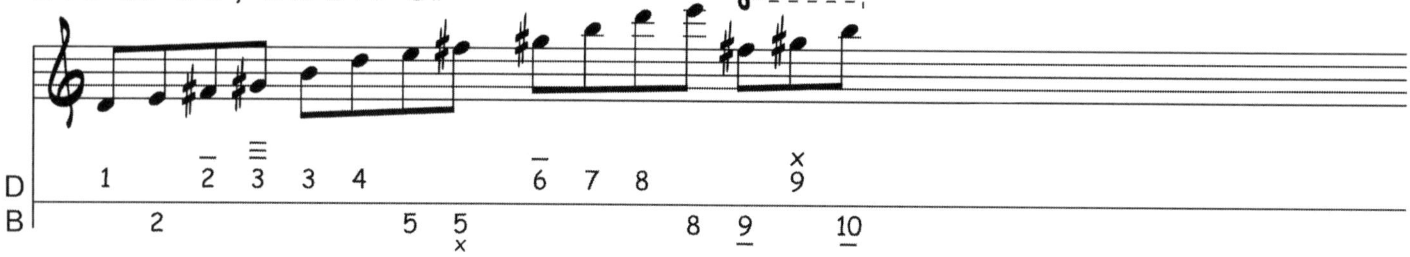

F G A C Eb / C Eb F G A

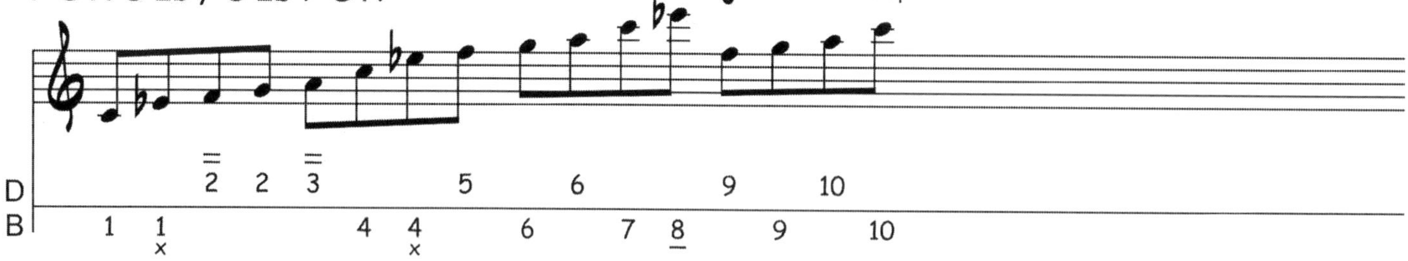

F# G# A# C# E / C# E F# G# A#

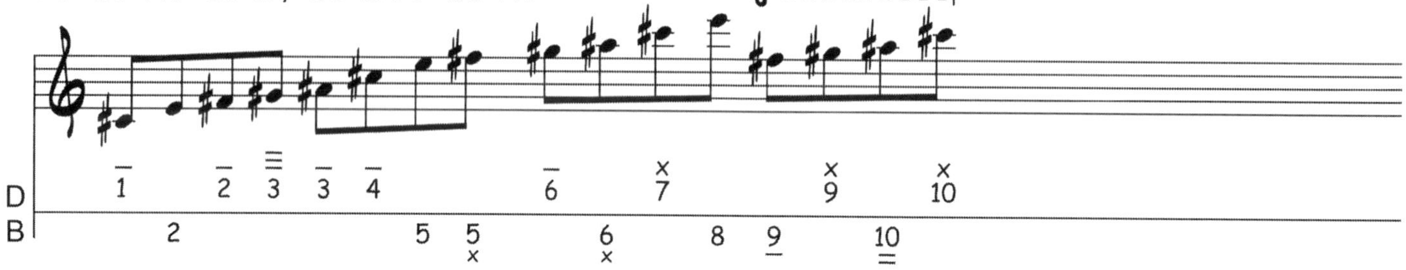

G A B D F / D F G A B

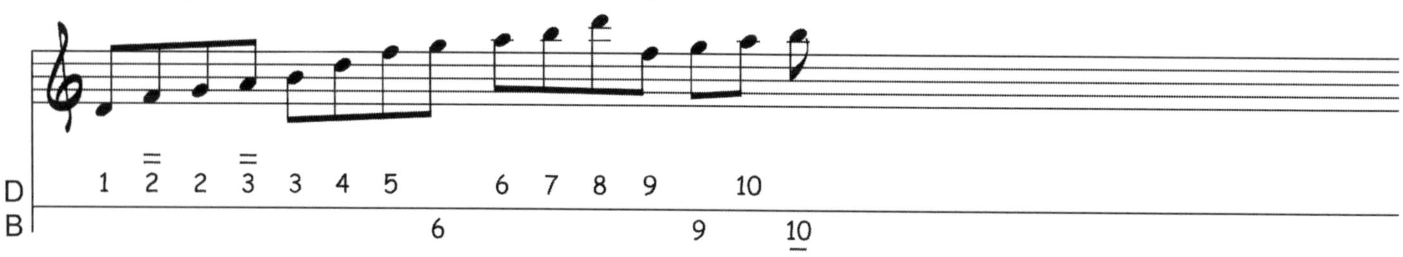

Ab Bb C Eb Gb / Eb Gb Ab Bb C

A B C# E G / E G A B C#

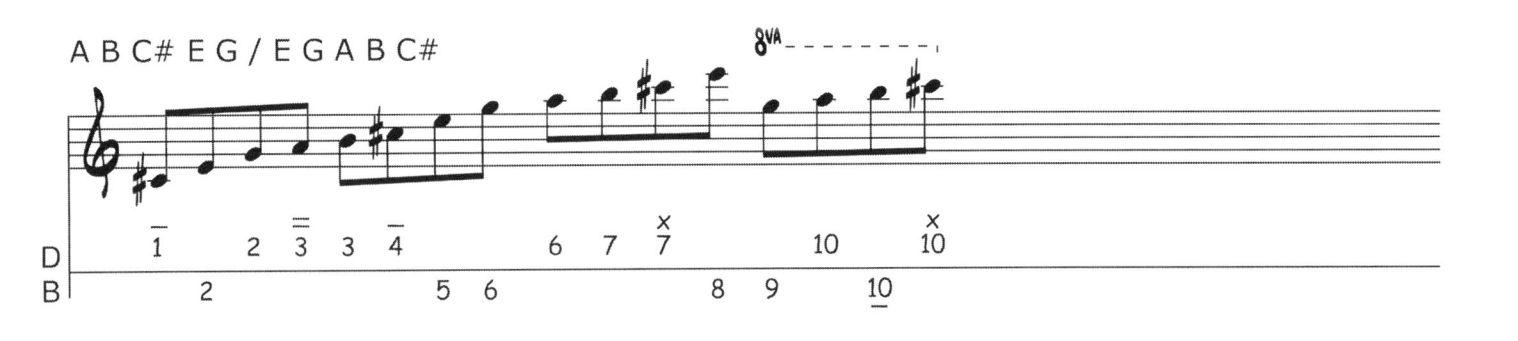

Bb C D F Ab / F Ab Bb C D

B C# D# F# A / F# A B C# D#

Harmonica School ©

55

Symmetrical Scales

Symmetrical scales are a category of their own. They are the most mathematical scales, they are based on a logic you can hear! The overall concept is that we are given 12 notes,
12 is a number you can divide by 1, 1.5, 2, 3, 4, 6 and 12.

So if we divide the octave by 1 or 12, we get the chromatic scale (series of half-tones).
If we divide by 2 we obtain the whole tone scale (series of tones)

If we divide by 3 we get 4 tonics, which are equal in the system. We get the diminished (or half-diminished) scale. We will also deduce corresponding chords (diminished and more) which repeat in a serie of minor thirds.
The scale is built on a serie of 1 tone + a half tone.
The diminished chord included in this scale is a series of 1.5 tones.

If we divide by 4 we get 3 tonics. Same concept as the diminished concept but this time the octave is divided by 3 * 2 tones. We have 3 major thirds creating a symmetric system. We attain the augmented chord as well as the augmented scale which is a series of minor third + half tone.

If we divide by 6 we have a perfect division of the octave. This is the Tri Tone: 2 * 3 tones **(#4/b5)**.

This is just an overview of symmetry in music, for more detail I suggest you read the works of **Olivier Messiaen** and **Nicolas Slonimsky** who both influenced a lot of improvisers and composers.

Chromatic

1b22b334b55b66b77

Ex: **CDbDEbEFGbGAbABbB**

The ***Chromatic Scale*** is the biggest symmetrical scale, dividing all 12 semi-tones into the smallest possible division. It is built on a series of half steps; any note can be a new root.

There are 12 chromatic scales which contain all the same notes.

The Chromatic Scale has 2 main uses:

1. It is used to fill gaps inside other scales in a lot of different ways.

    Ex: If we take CDEFGABC, we could play those chromaticisms:
    CDbDEFGbGABC, **EbDbD**, **CDDbBC**, **GGbFEAbGGbF**
    Then we wouldn't necessarily say we created a new scale, we would have just added chromaticity to it.

2. It is used as a 12-tone scale to improvise, or newly compose, over one **Tonic**, or in an even more free way without any specific root.

Whole Tone

123#4#5b7

Ex: **CDEF#G#Bb**

Debussy made this scale popular, and it is found in a lot of **Jazz** compositions too. This scale is a repetition of whole tones hence its name. Pick any note, move up a whole tone and keep going.

After the 6th note you'll be back to the first note. There are really only 2 whole tone scales that we could name C whole tone, and C# whole tone.

C: CDEF#G#Bb
C#: C#D#FGAB

We could also use the whole tone scale a half tone above the root (C# whole tone played over C) gives us: **b2b34567.**

The whole tone scale is made of 2 augmented triad, a whole tone apart.
Caug + D aug give us: **CEG#, DF#A# = C Whole Tone Scale**

But we also find **Eaug, F#aug, G# aug** and **A# aug.**

Any note of the scale can be considered a potential root and therefore, **C Whole Tone** is also **D, E, F#, G#** and **A#** Whole Tone and so on.

We mainly use this scale to play over a **7b5** chord or **7#5** with a flat 9, overall you can use it on any **V7** chord resolving to I such as in **G7** to **Cmin7** or **Cmaj7**.

If you remove the last note, b7, you create a pentatonic scale that can be used over a **Maj7#5** or **min6** chord (starting on the b3). It has a very clear signature to it and is better used sparsely.

Whole Tone

123b5b6b7

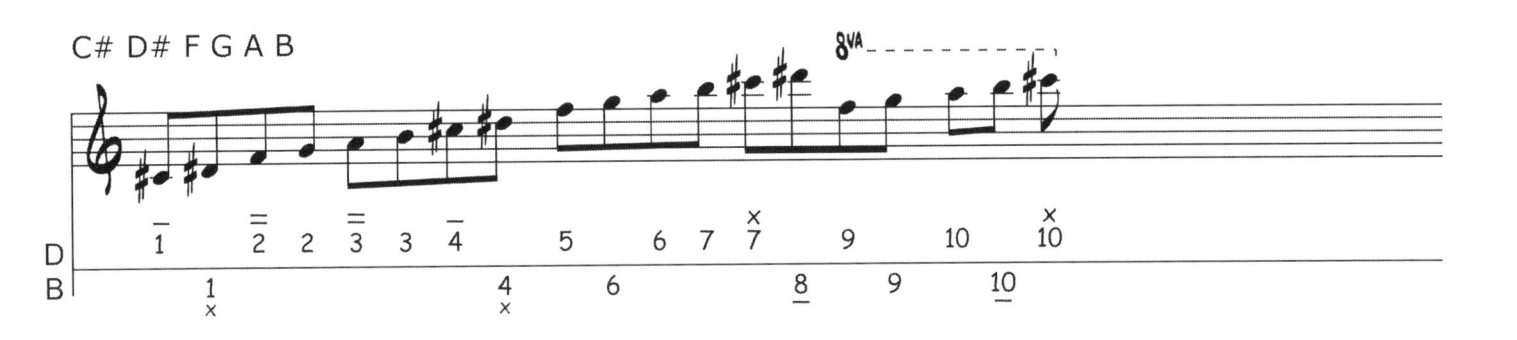

Half Diminished

1 b2 b3 3 b5 5 6 b7

Ex: **CDbEbEGbGABb**

It is an 8 Note Scale. If you start from the second note, you get the same scale usually called the **Diminished Scale**.

This scale is symmetrical and built on a repetitive series of half tone, tone, half tone, tone and so on so forth. So overall there are only 3 **Half Diminished Scales**, we could call them
C Half-Diminished, C# Half-Diminished, and **D Half-Diminished**.
As they repeat in a symmetrical way, there are really only 4 scales, or 4 **Tonics**, in each scale:
So **C** would also be **Eb**, **F#** and **A**.
C# is also **E, G** and **Bb**
D is also **F, Ab,** and **B**

It is a very interesting scale, which deserves a small book on its own. We find it most often employed over a **7b9**, **13b9** chord or the **dim7**, substitute for it.
Ex: **Edim7 (EGBbDb), Gdim7, Bbdim7, Dbdim7** can be a substitute to, **C7b9, Eb7b9, Gb7b9 or A7b9**. With **C Half-Diminished** we could then play over **C7b9, Eb7b9, F#7b9, A7b9, Dbdim7, Edim7, Gdim7, Bbdim7** and also why not over minor 7 static chords: **Cm7, Ebm7, F#m7**, and **Am7**.
We also find Cdim7, Ebdim, Gbdim7 and Adim7 in this same scale.

Watch out! On an altered chord, there is **NO 13!** And we would then prefer to use an altered scale to fit the chord.
Ex: On **C7b9** we can play both **C Half-Diminished** and **C altered**. But on **C7b9#5** the **#5** emphasizes the altered mode: **1b2b33b5b6b7** (or **C Mixolydian b9b13**)
On the opposite, **C13b9** urges us to use **C Half-Diminished** (or **C Mixolydian b9**)
Chord function depends on the harmonic context of the chord sequence, and this subject is beyond this books overall idea and focus. When in doubt, look at the written theme and use your ears!

C Eb F# A

C# E G Bb

D F Ab B

Half-Diminished
1b2b33#456b7

Augmented Scales

1 #2 3 5 b6 7

1 <u>2</u> b3 3 <u>#4</u> 5 b6 <u>b7</u> 7

EX : **CD#EGAbB**
9 Note : **CDEbEF#GAbBbB**

The augmented scale can be seen as the sum of 2 Augmented Triad, a minor 3rd apart:
C+ and **Eb+**.
CEG#, EbGB = CEbEG#GB

We also find 3 major triads a major 3rd apart:
C + E + Ab = CEG, EG#B, AbCEb

But we also find minor triads in the augmented scale!

3 minor triads **Cm**, **Em**, **G#m**:
CEbG, EGB, G#BD#

It is a very modern sounding scale; somewhat hard to manoeuver because of the multiplicity of chords involved, and the lack of clear definition of which one is more important. It is a symmetrical scale.

If we extend it to 7th chords and more, we always run into unfamiliar extensions.

Cmaj7 with a **#9**.
CminMaj7 with a **Major Third**.
As this scale is symmetrical, there are really only 4 augmented scales which yield the following formulas:

- <u>Augmented</u>: **1b335b67**
- <u>Mode 2</u>: **1b234#56**
- <u>1 Tone Higher (D Aug on C)</u>: **b224b56b7**
- <u>b3 higher (Eb Aug on C)</u>: **2b3b55b77**

The main uses are:

C Augmented on **Cmaj7** or **Calt**, **Balt**, **Bb13b9**. Also try it on **Amin7 static**. It is clearly easier to use it on a static chord, than in a progression.

The 9 note augmented scale is a regular augmented scale with extra notes.
Augmented Scale: 1#235b67, 9 note Augmented Scale: 1**2**b33**#4**5b6**b7**7
We add an Augmented Triad on the 2nd degree, or we add a note a half tone below the **b3**, the **5** and the **7**.

It is made of three Augmented Triads **C**, **B** and **Bb**: **CEG#, BD#G, BbDGb**.
Try to play **C** 9 note Augmented scale over:

- **Cmaj7#5, Calt, D7, Bb7, F#m7b5 and Am7**

At first, it will be easier to start using those chords on a static note.

This scale has been used by:
- **John Coltrane,**
- **Bob Berg,**
- **Michael Brecker,**
- **Frank Zappa**
- *But also, in a lot of films, or by Bela Bartok and the English composer, Gustav Holst.*

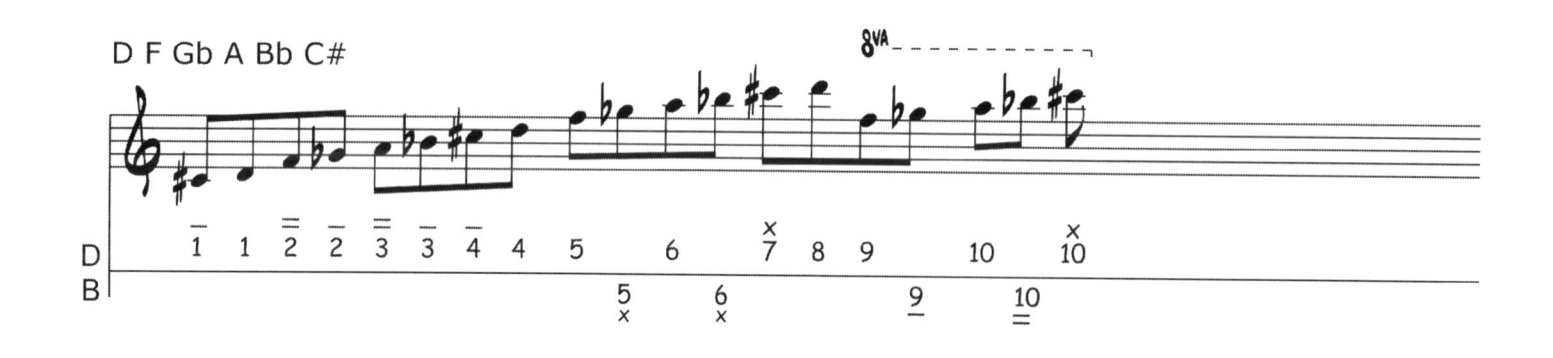

Augmented
1#235b67

9 notes Augmented
12b33#45b6b77

Harmonica school

C D Eb E F# G Ab Bb B

Db Eb E F G Ab A B C

D E F F# G# A A# C C#

Eb F F# G A A# B C# D

Harmonica School ©

Be-Bop Scales

Bebop Scales attract a bit of controversy, because, you can simply see them as major and minor scales with an extra chromaticism. This is why they are only listed in C as a reference, But you may prefer to learn the source scales first, and then simply work on adding chromaticisms.

So here are the scales broke down in a simpler way:

Major Bebop Scale: *12345#567*

CDEFF#GAB to be played over: **Cmaj7**.
This is a Major Scale with **#5** as a passing tone between the **5**th and the **6**th.
Can be seen as **Cmaj6** (CEGA) + **Ddim7** (DFAbB)

Dominant Bebop Scale: *123456b77*

CDEFGABbB to be played over: **C7**.
This scale is a **Mixolydian Mode** (*Major Scale Mode*) with a **7**th as a passing tone between the **b7**, and the **Tonic**.
Can be seen as **C7** (CEGBb) + **Ddim7** (DFAbB)

Minor Bebop Scale: *12b345b667*

CDEbFGAbAB, to be played over: **Cm6** and **CmMaj7**.
This scale is a **Melodic Minor Scale** with a b6 as a passing tone between the **5**th and the **6**th.
Can be seen as **Cm6** (CEbGA) + **Ddim7** (DFAbB)

Minor Bebop Scale 2: *12b345b66b7*

CDEbFGAbABb, to be played over: **Cm7**.
This scale is in **Dorian Mode** (*Major Scale Mode*), with a **b6** as a passing tone between the **5**th and the **6**th.

Dominant Altered Bebop Scale: *1b2345b6b77*

CDbEFGAbBbB, to be played over: **C7b9b13**.
This scale is a **Mixolydian b2b6 Scale** (*5*th *mode of the Harmonic Minor Mode*) with a **7**th as a passing tone between the **b7** and the **Tonic**.

Bebop Scales

harmonica school

Dominant altered bebop scale : 1b2b33b5b6b77

Extra Scales

There are even more scales!

As stated in the beginning, it is easy to create scales, but with the material provided in this book you have a very complete collection of useful scales, and those bonus scales are an opening to an even larger scope in case you get bored with the previous ones, or maybe let your curious side take over. Remember, that in traditional music some of the regular scales might be called by a different name.

In this chapter I will explain and detail some other extra scales that you might want to explore or understand.

Persian Scale: 1b234b5b67

CDbEFGbAbB: Very close to the second mode of a double minor harmonic scale, only one note is different; F Double Harmonic Minor: C Db E F **G** Ab B

Enigmatic Scale: 1b23b5b6b7

CDbEGbAbBb: We can see it as an altered scale (7th mode of Melodic Minor) without a b3. It was used by Verdi, and sounds good to replace the altered scale.

Messiaen 5th Mode: 1b24b557

CDbFGbGB: The French composer **Messiaen** developed a system of limited transposition scales, those scales are part of the symmetrical family made of 2 sus triads (Csus and Gb sus), usable over a sus **maj7** chord, to create a specific sound or be used to play out.

Messiaen 6th Mode: 1234b5b6b7 7

CDEFF#G#A#B: Can be seen as a blend of two major scales, **C** and **F#**.
1234 of C+**1234** of **F#**. C and F# are a triton apart and share only two notes (**B** and **F**).
We find two augmented triads in this scale: **C+** and **D+** and **Dm7b5**, **C7#5**. Can be useful to play over augmented chords or to create tensions over a static chord.

Prometheus Scale: 123#46b7

Modern sounding this is simply a **Lydian b7** Scale without a 5th. Sounds good to replace the **Lydian b7** Scale, or inversed to replace the **Melodic Minor Scale**.

Arabian Scale: 1234b5b6b7

This is the same as **Messiaen** 6th mode without the major 7th.
Gives an **F# triad over C** chord very altered sound, play over **C7b5**.

Hungarian Major: 1#23#456b7

Same as the 6th mode of double harmonic minor but with a 6th instead of a major 7th, try it over a 7#9 chord.

8 Note Spanish: 1b2b334b5b6b7 (Altered)

Same as the altered mode (7th of melodic minor), with an extra chromatic between the 3rd major and the **b5**. Sounds good when replacing the altered mode.

Extra Scales

Persian : 1 b2 3 4 b5 5 b6 7

Enigmatic scale : 1 b2 3 b5 b6 b7

Messiaen 5th mode : 1 b2 4 b5 5 7

Messiaen 6th Mode : 1 2 3 4 b5 b6 b7 7

Prometheus : 123#46b7

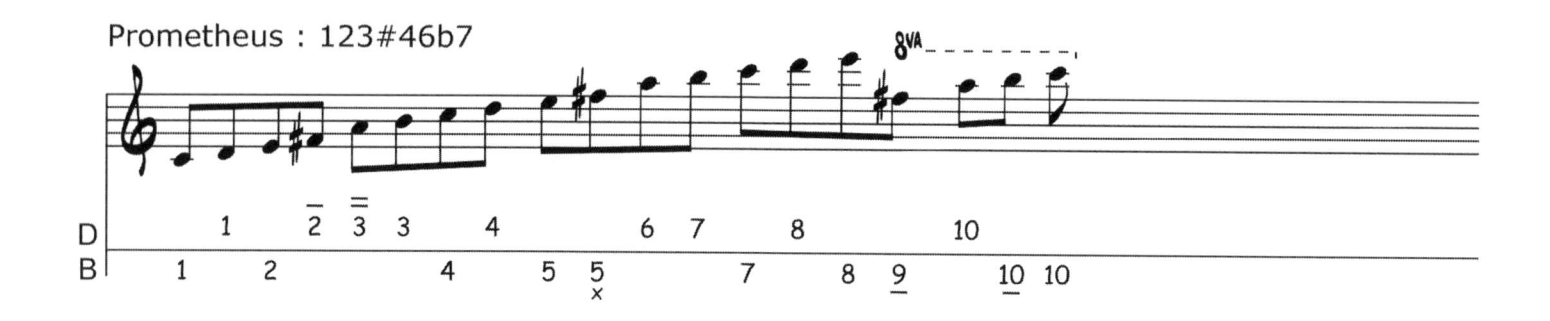

Arabian : 1234b5b6b7

8 note spanish : 1b2b334b5b6b7 (altered)

Hungarian major : 1#23#456b7

Harmonica School ©

Extra Pentatonic Scales

Here are some Extra Pentatonic Scales:

It is so easy to build a pentatonic scale and there are so many options! I decided to introduce you to some other, though less frequently used Pentatonic Scales, as well as a few personal ones. I hope you will enjoy their sound.

Below are the intervallic formulas as well as comments:

Major b2 Pentatonic Scale: 1b2356

CDbEGA plays over **C7**, **Eb7**, **F#7**, and **A7**.

Major b6 Pentatonic: 1235b6

CDEGAb plays over **FmMaj7**, **Ealt**, **Bb7#11**, and **G#Maj7**.

Indian Scale: 1b245b6

CDbFGAb

Used by the Newgrass Revival band in one of their composition Sapporo, this scale from India is a nice choice over a minor chord. It is a light version of the **Phrygian** mode, and you can thus substitute it to the **Phrygian** mode.

Personnal Pentatonics:

Min Maj7 Pentatonic: 1b3457

CEbFGB: substitute to any melodic or harmonic minor scale, and all of their modes. The m6 pentatonic is Melodic Minor Scale related, whereas the mMaj7 can be Melodic or Harmonic Minor Scale related since it has no specific unshared note.

Use it on **Cm6**, **CmMaj7**, **B7alt**, **F7#11**, **Ebmaj7#5**, **G7b13**, **G7b9b13**, **Am7b5**, **Dm7b5**.

Dominant Blues: 1345b7

CEFGBb: sounds good over a 7th chord with a typical bluesy feel, it is also compatible with the **Mixolydian b9b13** mode.

Try it over **C7**, **Gm7**, **G7b9b13**.

Lydian Pentatonic: 12#457

CDF#GB: Ideal to make a Maj7 chord sound **Lydian**, try it on **Cmaj7#11**.

7b9 Pentatonic: 1b235b7

CDbEGBb: Built from the half-diminished scale, this scale sounds good on **7b9**, and **13b9** chords. This also sounds very good on a diminished 7th chord, starting the scale from the 7th.
Ex: For **Bbdim7,** play **C7b9 Pentatonic**
As the half-diminished scale is symmetrical you can transpose the usage up to 4 different tonics. Therefore you can play **C7b9** Pentatonic over **C7b9**, **Eb7b9**, **F#7b9**, **A7b9**
Bbdim7, **Dbdim7**, **Edim7**, and **Gdim7.**

7b5b9 Pentatonic: 1b23b5b7

CdbEGbBb: Also built from the half-diminished scale, this scale will sound amazing on a **7b5b9** chord, or this altered chord: **C7b9#5**.

Use the **C7b9b5** Pentatonic on **C7b5b9**, **Eb7b9b5**, **F#7b9b5**, **A7b9b5**, **Bbdim7**, **Dbdim7**, **Edim7**, and **Gdim7.**

Extra Pentatonic

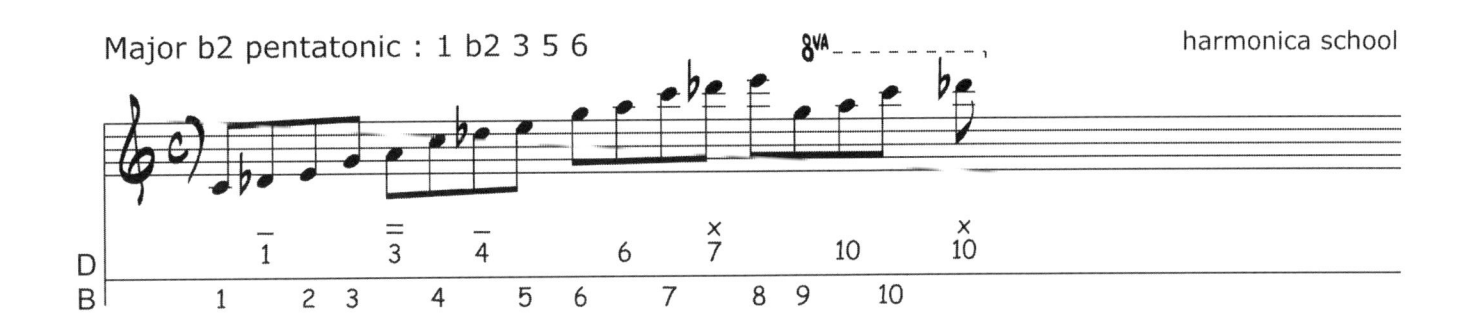

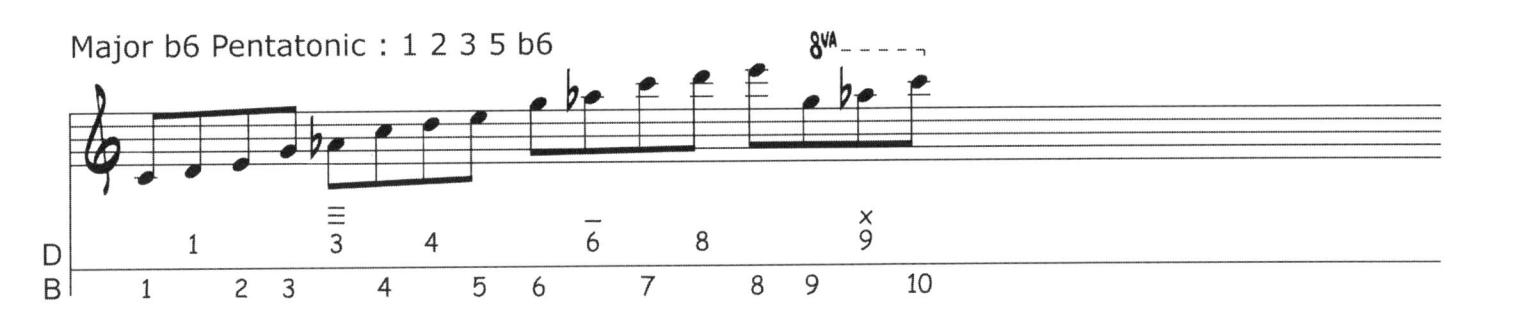

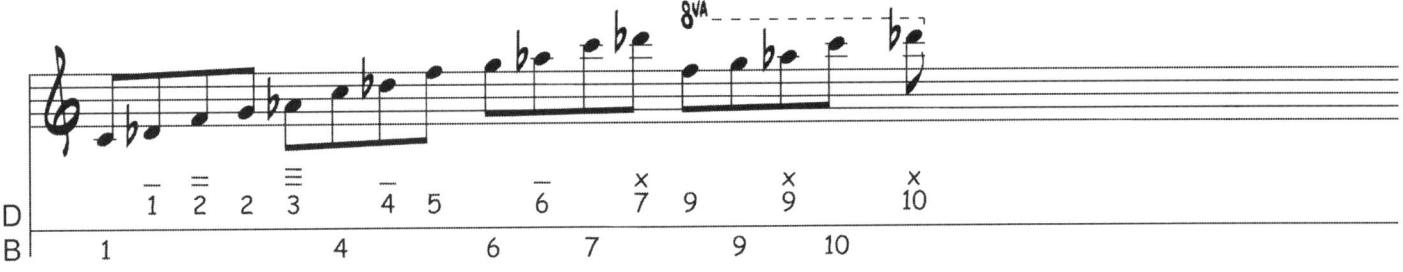

Blues dominant Pentatonic : 1 3 4 5 b7

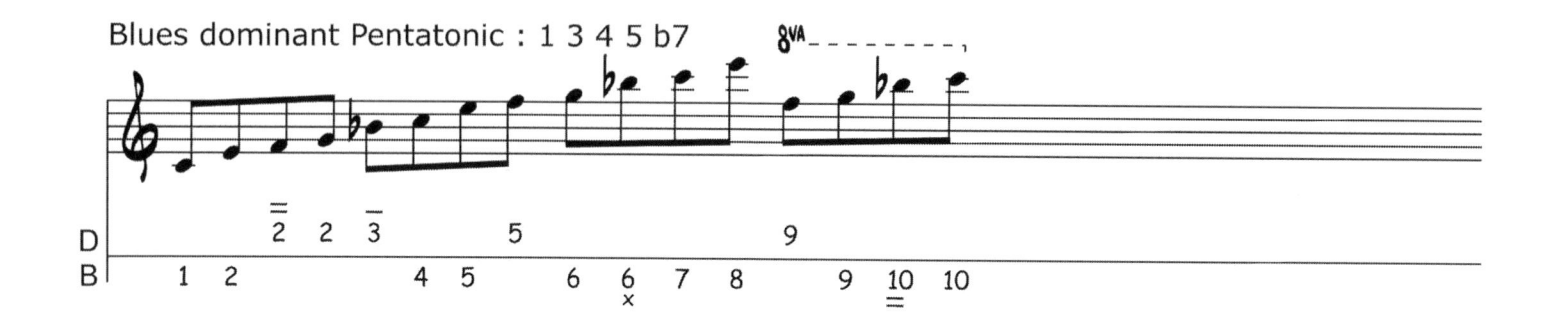

Major 7th / Lydian Pentatonic : 1 2 #4 5 7

7b9 Pentatonic : 1 b2 3 5 b7 diminished start on b7

7b5b9 Pentatonic : 1 b2 3 b5 b7

Harmonica School ©

Scales and Modes Reference Sheet

Major Scales and Modes:

Ionian : 1234657
Dorian : 12b3456b7
Phrygian : 1b2b34b5b6b7
Lydian : 123#4567
Mixolydian : 123456b7
Aeolian : 12b345b6b7
Locrian : 1b2b34b5b6b7

Melodic Minor Scales and Modes:

Minor Melodic: 12b34567
Dorian b2: 1b23456b7
Lydian #5: 123#4#567
Lydian b7: 123#456b7
Mixolydian b6: 12345b6b7
Locrian #2: 12b34b5b6b7
Altered: 1b2b33b5b6b7

Harmonic Minor Scale and Modes:

Harmonic minor : 12b345b67
Locrian#6 : 1b2b34b56b7
Ionian augmented : 1234#567
Dorian#4 : 12b3#456b7
Mixolydianb2b6: 1b2345b6b7
Lydian#2 : 1#23#4567
Diminished : 1b2b33b5b66

Harmonic Major Scale and Modes:

Harmonic Major: 12345b67
Dorian b5: 12b34b56b7
Phrygian b4: 1b2b335b6b7
Lydian b3: 12b3#4567
Mixolydian b2: 1b23456b7
Lydian Augmented #2: 1#23#4#567
Locrian Diminished: 1b2b34b5b66

Double Harmonic Minor Scale and Modes:

Double Minor: 12b3#45b67
Oriental: 1b234b56b7
3rd Mode: 1b334#567
4th Mode: 1b224b5b66
Double Harmonic Major: 1b2345b67
6th Mode: 1#23#45b77
7th Mode: 1b2b335b66

Pentatonic Major/Minor:

Major: 12356
Mode 2: 1245b7
Mode 3: 1b34b6b7
Mode 4: 12456
Mode 5/Minor: 1b345b7

Pentatonic Dominant/Minor 6:

Dominant: 1235b7
Mode 2: 124b6b7
Mode 3: 1b3b5b6b7
Minor 6: 1b3456
Mode 5: 123#46

m7b5 Pentatonic:

m7b5: 1b34b5b7
Japanese: 12b356
Mode 3: 1b245b7
Mode 4: 13b567
Mode 5: 1245b6

Pentatonic Major b6 :

Maj b6: 1235b6
Mode 2: 124b5b7
Mode 3: 1b33b6b7
Mode 4: 1b2456
Mode 5: 13b5b67

Whole Tone:

123#4#5b7
Half Tone Higher: b2b34567

Half-diminished:

Half-dimished: 1b2b33b556b7
Diminished: 12b34b5b667
Augmented:
Augmented: 1b335b67
Mode 2: 1b234#56
Half Tone Higher: b22b3b56b7
Higher b3: 2b3b55b77

9 Scale Augmented:

Mode 1: 12b33#45#5b77
Mode 2: 1b2234b5b66b7
Mode 3: 1b2b3345#567

Bebop Scales:

Major Bebop Scale: 12345#567
Dominant Bebop Scale: 123456b77
Minor Bebop Scale: 12b345b667
Minor Bebop Scale 2: 12b345b66b7
Dominant Altered Bebop Scale: 1b2345b6b77

Extra Scales:

Gamme Perse: 1b234b5b67
Enigmatic Scale: 1b23b5b6b7
Messiaen 5th Mode: 1b24b557
Messiaen 6th Mode: 1234b5b6b77
Arabian: 1234b5b6b7
Prometheus: 123#46b7
8 Note Spanish: 1b2b334b5b6b7 (altered)
Six Tone Symmetrical: 1b234#567
Hungarian Major: 1#23#456b7

Extra Pentatonics :

Major b2: 1b2356
Major b6: 1235b6
Hindu: 1b245b6
Min/Maj 7: 1b3457
Dominant Blues: 1345b7
Lydian: 12#457
Penta 7b9: 1b235b7
Penta 7b5b9: 1b23b5b7

Chord / Scale Relationship

It is a very broad subject, so please find below an un-complete, but practical list of each main chord. You can see the chord type as well as the related scales to play over.

Please be aware that choices may vary depending on the chord function inside a chord progression. In order to get more familiar with the scale sound over a chord, it would be a good idea to practice those scales over a static chord first, and in an usual progression later (ii V I, I VI ii V...)

To simplify learning those modes, I also wrote in brackets from which note of the main related scale you should start.

Ex: For a Maj7 chord, if we play the **Major Scale** starting on the 5th of the chord, we get the **Lydian** mode. In the list it is then written **Lydian** and its formula 123#4567, as well as (5 major scale) meaning: On a Maj7 chord play the **Major Scale** from the fifth (5) to get the **Lydian** mode.

Concerning **Pentatonics,** I simplified even more, just showing on which degree to start.
More options are possible and you can add to the list, of course this is overall a matter of taste and context. Choices with a lot of altered notes will be harder to use. If you play **Modern Jazz**, your options will be different than if you play **Pop**.

7 chord category address static **7** or **7#11** chord, whereas **alt7** chord is for any **V7** chord resolving to **I**.

Maj7 :

Ionian 1234657

Lydian 123#4567 (5 Major)

Major Pentatonic on 1: 12356

Major Pentatonic on 2: 234#67

Major Pentatonic on 5: 23567

Dominant Pentatonic on 2: 123#46

Dominant Pentatonic on 3: 23#4#57

m7b5 Pentatonic on #4: 13#467

Majb6 Pentatonic on 1: 1235b6

Majb6 Pentatonic on 3: 13b5b67

Ionian Augmented: 1234#567 (6 Harmonic Minor)

Lydian #5: 123#4#567 (6 Melodic Minor)

Lydian #4: 1#23#4567 (3 Melodic Minor)

Lydian b3: 12b3#4567 (5 Melodic Minor)

Double harmonic major: 1b2345b67 (4 Double Harmonic Minor)

Augmented: 1b335b67

9 notes Augmented: 12b33#45#5b77

Double Harmonic Minor 3rd Mode: 1b334#567 (6 Double Harmonic Minor)

min 7:

Dorian: 12b3456b7 (b7 Major)

Minor Pentatonic on 1: 1b345b7

Minor Pentatonic on 2: 12456

Minor Pentatonic on 5: 1245b7

(= Major Pentatonic on b3 4 and b7)

Minor 6 Pentatonic: 1b3456

Japanese: 12b356 (6 m7b5 Pentatonic)

Phrygian: 1b2b34b5b6b7 (b6 Major)

Aeolien: 12b345b6b7 (b3 Major)

Melodic Minor: 12b34567

Harmonica Minor: 12b345b67

Dorian#4: 12b3#456b7 (5 Harmonic Minor)

Dorianb5: 12b34b56b7 (5 Harmonic Major)

Double Harmonic Minor: 12b3#45b67

m7b5:

Locrian: 1b2b34b5b6b7 (b2 Major)

m7b5 Pentatonic: 1b34b5b7

Major Pentatonic on b5: b2b3b5b6b7

Major Pentatonic on b6: 1b34b6b7

Dominant pentatonic on b6: 1b3b5b6b7

Locrian#2: 12b34b5b6b7 (6 Melodic Minor)

7:

Mixolydian: 123456b7 (4 major)

Lydian b7: 123#456b7 (5 melodic minor)

Major Pentatonic on 1: 12356

Major Pentatonic on b5: b23b5b6b7

Major Pentatonic on b6: 1b34b6b7

Dominant Pentatonic on 1: 1235b7

Dominant Pentatonic on 2: 123#46

7Alt :

Major Pentatonic on b5: b2b3b5b6b7

Dominant Pentatonic on b5: b23b5b6b7

Dominant Pentatonic on b6: 1b3b5b6b7

Mixolydianb6: 12345b6b7 (4 melodic minor)

Altered: 1b2b33b5b6b7 (b2 melodic minor)

Mixolydian b2b6: 1b2345b6b7 (4 harmonic minor)

Phrygianb4 : 1b2b335b6b7 (b6 harmonic major)

Major Pentatonic b9: b2b34b6b7

Major Pentatonic b3: 1b345b7

Major Pentatonic on b6: 1b34b6b7

Oriental: 1b234b56b7 (b7 double harmonic minor)

Whole Tone: 123#4#5b7

Half-Diminished: 1b2b33b556b7

Augmented on 1, b2 and 2

Diatonic Tab System

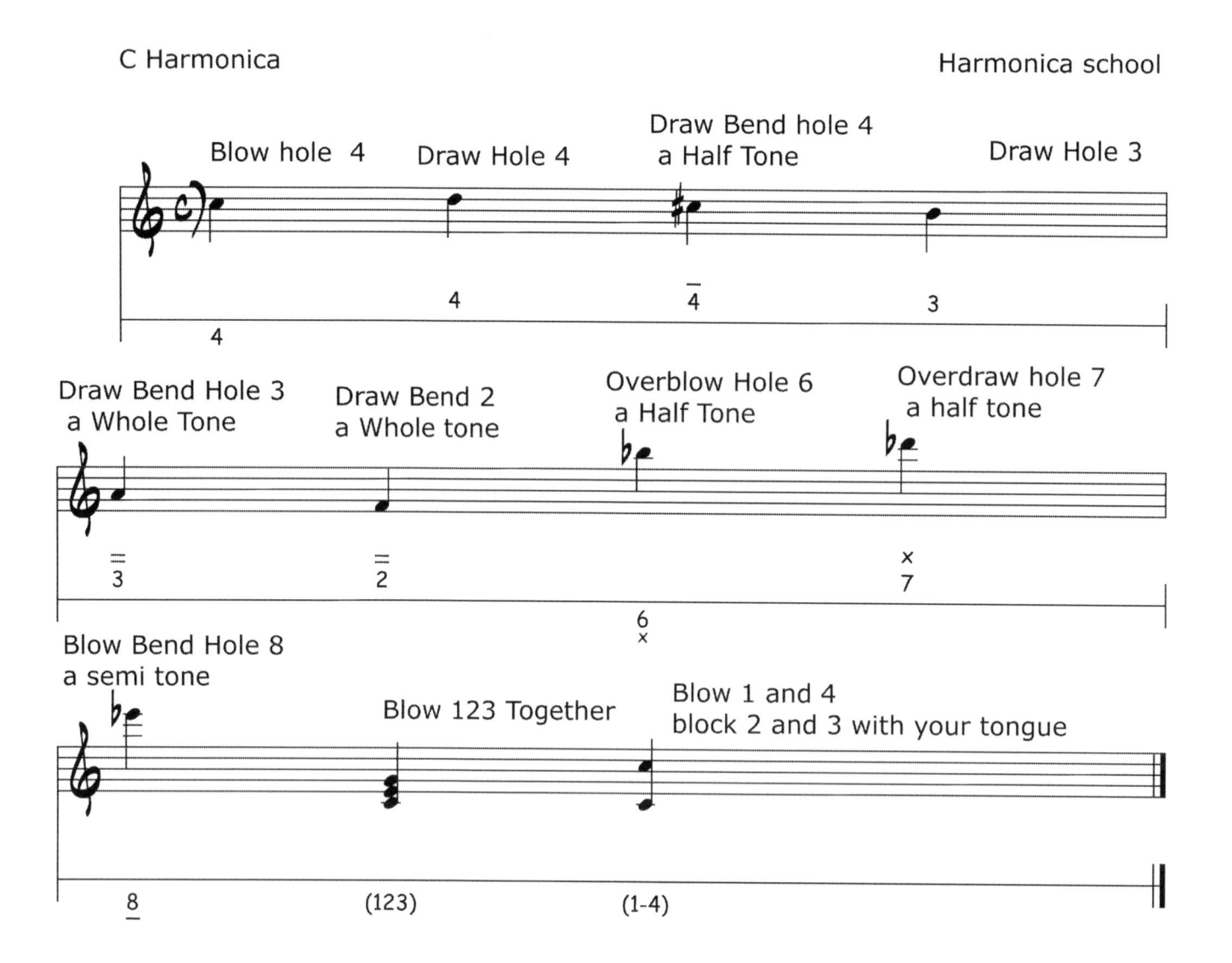

C Harmonica   Harmonica school

- Blow hole 4 — 4
- Draw Hole 4 — 4̄
- Draw Bend hole 4 a Half Tone — 4̄ (with bend marking)
- Draw Hole 3 — 3
- Draw Bend Hole 3 a Whole Tone — 3̿
- Draw Bend 2 a Whole tone — 2̿
- Overblow Hole 6 a Half Tone — 6 ×
- Overdraw hole 7 a half tone — 7 ×
- Blow Bend Hole 8 a semi tone — 8 (underlined)
- Blow 123 Together — (123)
- Blow 1 and 4 block 2 and 3 with your tongue — (1-4)